modern classics BOOK 2

about the author

Donna Hay is an Australian-based food stylist, author, food writer and magazine editor. Her two most recent cookbooks, *modern classics book 1* and *off the shelf*, published with HarperCollins, are bestsellers, and *donna hay* magazine, launched in 2001 with News Magazines, is a continuing popular success. She also has a weekly Australia-wide newspaper column and is well known for the four cookbooks she produced for *marie claire* – *marie claire cooking*, *marie claire dining*, *marie claire food fast* and *marie claire flavours* (published internationally as *The New Cook*, *New Entertaining*, *New Food Fast* and *Flavours*, respectively) – which have brought her global success. Awards and nominations to date: for *modern classics book 1*, Gourmand World Cookbook Awards (Spain) 2002 – Best Cookbook Design in the World. For *off the shelf*, Gourmand World Cookbook Awards (Spain) – Best Design Book in English. For *food fast*, Jacob's Creek World Food Media Awards (Aus) – Silver Award, Best Soft Cover Recipe Book 2001; The Vittoria Australian Food Writers' Awards (Aus) – Food Media Club Australia Award for Best Soft Cover Recipe Book 2001. For *flavours*, The Guild of Food Writers Awards 2000 (UK) – Cookery Book of the Year; Glenfiddich Award (UK) – Best Cook Book 2001; James Beard Foundation/Kitchen Aid Book Awards (USA) – nominee for Best Food Photography 2001. For *dining*, Jacob's Creek World Food Media Awards (Aust) – Gold Award – Best Soft Cover Recipe Book 1999; Australian Food Writers' Award 1999 (Aust) for Best Soft Cover Recipe Book. For *cooking*, International Association of Culinary Professionals Cookbook Awards (USA) (formerly the Julia Child Cookbook Awards) – The Design Award 1998.

thank you

Producing my books has always involved calling on the talents of many. Never more so than with this one. With a new baby and a bimonthly magazine happening at the same time, my schedule was seriously challenged and this book would never have made it to the printer without the help of these incredible people. Creative director Vanessa Holden – genius designer, time-keeper, schedule-maker and all-round miracle-worker; a million thanks. Photographer Con Poulos – award-winning winemaker and accomplished lamb spit-roaster and tomato-sauce bottler, your passion for food really does shine through in your photographs; thanks also for the laughs and friendship. The amazing kitchen team of Sonia Greig, Emma Knowles, Kate Murdoch and Justine Poole – I know that testing the same recipe six or so times until it's absolutely perfect isn't exactly your idea of fun, so thanks for your patience, persistence and passion. Prop sylist Vanessa Morris – I dream of a prop and you find it; thank you for adding so much more. Editor Lucy Tumanow-West – thank you for the beautiful words and for twisting this book into shape, all while bouncing Olivia on your knee. Thank you to our produce suppliers – The Antico Boys and Murdoch Produce – and prop suppliers – The Peppertree Berrima, Le Creuset, Pillyvut @ Hale Imports, Art of Wine and Food, Panton Enterprises, Stoneage Ceramics, Wedgwood, Villeroy and Boch, Detpak, Lygon Imports, Callebaut Chocolate, David Jones, Design Mode International and Major and Tom – and kitchen suppliers – KitchenAid, Damien @ Sunbeam, Tony Lee @ Smeg Appliances, Profiline Cookware, Chef's Warehouse. Last, but by no means least, a huge thank you to Bill for your support in these mildly busy and frantic times.

First published in Australia in 2003
by HarperCollins*Publishers* Pty Limited
First published in Great Britain in 2003
by Fourth Estate
A Division of HarperCollinsPublishers
77–85 Fulham Palace Road
London W6 BJB
www.4thestate.com

1 3 5 7 9 10 8 6 4 2

A catalogue record for this book is available from the British Library.

ISBN 0 00 714907 7

Cover photograph: Almond cakes with sugared raspberries. For recipe, see page 62
Film by Colorwize Studios, Adelaide, South Australia
Produced in Hong Kong by Phoenix Offset on 157gsm Chinese Matt Art
Printed in China

modern classics book 2

donna hay

photography by con poulos

FOURTH ESTATE • *London*

contents

introduction

What makes something a classic? The way it endures the test of time, staying popular even when fashions change. With recipes, there are certain cakes people always ask for, particular tarts they can't go past, and favourite puddings that never fail to please. Quite often these will be recipes from another era – bombe Alaska, bread and butter pudding, date loaf, lemon meringue pie – or contemporary ones that have classic written all over them (orange poppyseed cake and tiramisu both spring to mind).

This book is my interpretation of the modern classics of the cake and dessert world. Some of the choices are obvious. Apple pie, crème caramel and shortbread, for example. And some recipes I have modified to bring in line with the way we do things now, such as my take on summer pudding and trifle. But however they look now, many of the ideas have come from the old commonsense cookery book my grandma gave me when I was only 10 years old. It's a treasured possession, and one of my fondest memories is of days spent in the kitchen with Grandma, learning the cooking basics that still serve me so well today.

If you can make these recipes, you don't need to know how to make anything else. At the same time, if you can make these recipes, you can make anything. That was my twofold aim in producing the *modern classics* cookbooks – to create a modern version of the reliable old commonsense cookery approach, and to give people a range of easy yet interesting recipes that will inspire confidence in the kitchen no matter what a person's age or cooking expertise. Please note that there is an explanation of ingredients and methods marked with an asterisk in the Glossary at the back of the book. Details of any cake tins or other bakingware marked with an asterisk can be found in the Tools section at the back of the book.

These are the cakes and cookies, biscuits and slices, pies and tarts, desserts and puddings everyone wants to know how to make. The sweets of our dreams. Enjoy making those dreams come true in the tastiest of ways.

Donna

cookies, biscuits + slices

tasty

tempting

irresistible.

The snap and dunkability of a crisp little biscuit. The sensational flavour and texture contrasts of a freshly made slice. A lusciously chewy cookie with its incredibly crunchy base. I've made it one of my aims in life for the art of biscuit, slice and cookie making never to be lost. Because the only thing that could bring more joy and satisfaction than seeing a jar of jam drops you've made yourself perched on the kitchen bench is to dip one into a steaming cup of tea and pop it in your mouth. The same with the all-at-once creaminess and flakiness of a homemade vanilla slice. As the incredibly smooth custard centre oozes between sticky sweet fingers and into eager mouths, you'll understand why my passion for making shortbread and anzacs, melting moments and chocolate chip cookies is not a thing of the past. So get ready to bake and enjoy plenty of your old favourites and a few great new ones that I just know are bound for the sweet treats hall of fame.

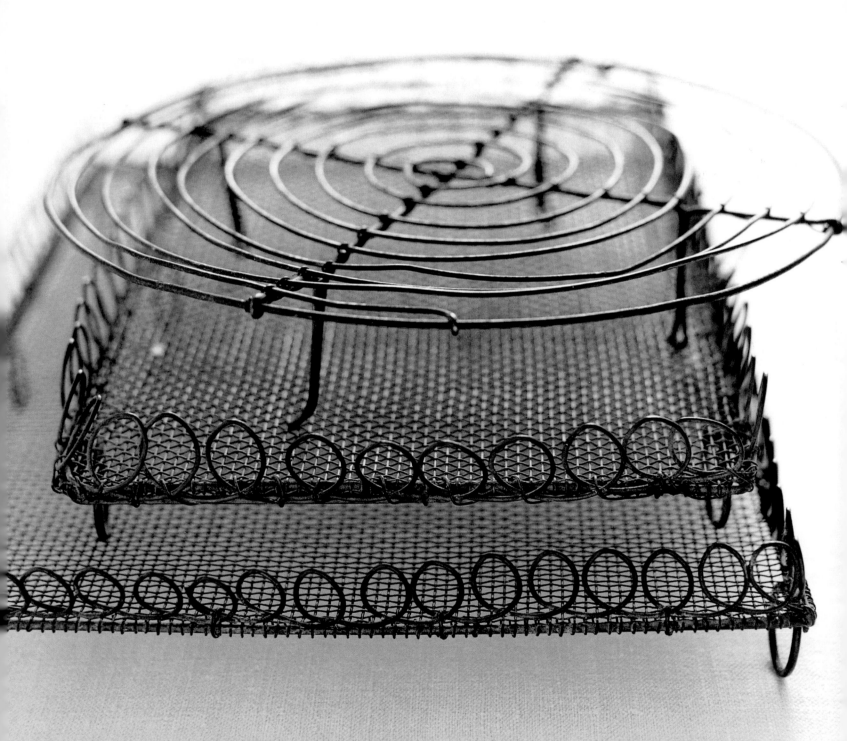

how to shortbread

220g (7 1/2 oz) chilled butter, chopped
2/3 cup caster (superfine) sugar
2 cups plain (all-purpose) flour
1/2 cup rice flour
1 teaspoon vanilla extract
1 egg

Preheat the oven to 160°C (325°F). Process the butter, sugar, flour, rice flour, vanilla and egg in a food processor until a smooth dough forms.

Place the dough on a lightly floured surface and knead gently.

Press the mixture into a 20cm x 30cm (8 in x 12 in) slice tin lined with non-stick baking paper. Smooth the surface with the back of a spoon and score the top into long bars. Bake for 1 hour or until golden. Cool in the tin. Slice along the score marks. Makes 22 slices.

individual shortbread biscuits **Roll tablespoons of the dough into balls. Place on baking trays lined with non-stick baking paper and flatten slightly with a fork. Bake at 160ºC (325ºF) for 22–25 minutes or until just golden brown.**
lemon shortbread **Omit the vanilla extract and knead 1 tablespoon finely grated lemon rind into the dough after processing in step 1.**
ginger shortbread **Omit the vanilla extract and knead 1/4 cup (90g/3 oz) finely chopped glacé ginger into the dough after processing in step 1.**
lavender shortbread **Omit the vanilla extract and knead 1 1/2 tablespoons washed and dried lavender buds into the dough after processing in step 1.**

shortbread slices and biscuits

13

oaty anzac biscuits

chocolate chip cookies

chocolate-filled biscuits

oaty anzac biscuits

1 cup rolled oats
1 cup plain (all-purpose) flour
1/2 cup sugar
3/4 cup desiccated coconut
2 tablespoons golden syrup
125g (4 oz) butter
1/2 teaspoon bicarbonate of soda (baking soda)
1 tablespoon hot water

Preheat the oven to 160°C (325°F). Place the oats, flour, sugar and coconut in a bowl. Place the golden syrup and butter in a saucepan over low heat and allow to melt. Mix the bicarbonate of soda with the water and add to the butter mixture. Pour the butter mixture into the dry ingredients and mix well.
Place tablespoonfuls of the mixture on baking trays lined with non-stick baking paper, allowing room for the biscuits to spread, and flatten slightly. Bake for 10 minutes or until golden. Cool on wire racks. Makes 22.

chocolate chip cookies

125g (4 oz) butter, softened
1/2 teaspoon vanilla extract
1 cup brown sugar
2 eggs
2 cups plain (all-purpose) flour, sifted
1 teaspoon baking powder
1 cup desiccated coconut
185g (6 oz) milk or dark chocolate, broken into chunks

Preheat the oven to 190°C (375°F). Place the butter, vanilla and sugar in a bowl and beat until creamy. Beat in the eggs. Stir through the flour, baking powder, coconut and chocolate.
Roll tablespoonfuls of the mixture into balls. Place on baking trays lined with non-stick baking paper, allowing room for the cookies to spread, and flatten slightly. Bake for 10–12 minutes or until lightly browned. Makes 38.

chocolate-filled biscuits

65g (2 oz) cold butter, chopped
1/4 cup icing (confectioner's) sugar
1/2 cup plain (all-purpose) flour
2 1/2 teaspoons cornflour (cornstarch)
1 tablespoon cocoa powder
1 egg yolk

Preheat the oven to 180°C (350°F). Process the butter, icing sugar, flour, cornflour, cocoa and egg yolk in a food processor until a soft dough forms. Wrap in plastic wrap and refrigerate for 30 minutes.
Roll teaspoonfuls of the mixture into balls, place on baking trays lined with non-stick baking paper and flatten slightly. Bake for 5–7 minutes or until the bases are lightly cooked. Cool on trays.
Sandwich the biscuits with chocolate ganache (page 36). Makes 22 filled biscuits.

chocolate caramel slice

1 cup plain (all-purpose) flour
1/2 cup desiccated coconut
1/2 cup brown sugar
125g (4 oz) butter, melted
caramel filling
1/3 cup golden syrup
125g (4 oz) butter, melted
2 x 400g (14 oz) cans sweetened condensed milk
chocolate topping
185g (6 oz) dark chocolate
3 teaspoons vegetable oil

Preheat the oven to 180°C (350°F). Place the flour, coconut, sugar and butter in a bowl and mix well. Press the mixture into a 20cm x 30cm (8 in x 12 in) slice tin lined with non-stick baking paper and bake for 15–18 minutes or until brown.
To make the caramel filling, place the golden syrup, butter and condensed milk in a saucepan over low heat and stir for 7 minutes or until the caramel has thickened slightly. Pour over the cooked base and bake for 20 minutes or until the caramel is golden. Refrigerate the slice until cold. To make the chocolate topping, place the chocolate and oil in a saucepan over low heat and stir until melted. Remove from the heat and allow to cool slightly before spreading over the slice. Refrigerate until firm and cut into slices. Makes 24 slices.

chocolate caramel slice

jam drops

180g (6 oz) butter, softened
1 cup caster (superfine) sugar
1 egg
2 cups plain (all-purpose) flour, sifted
1/2 teaspoon baking powder
jam (jelly) to decorate

Preheat the oven to 180°C (350°F). Place the butter and
sugar in the bowl of an electric mixer and beat until light
and creamy. Add the egg and beat well. Stir through the
flour and baking powder and mix to a dough.
Roll 2 teaspoonfuls of the mixture into balls. Place on
a baking tray lined with non-stick baking paper, allowing
room for the biscuits to spread, and flatten slightly. Press
a finger into the middle of the dough to make an indent.
Fill the hole with jam. Bake for 10 minutes or until golden.
Add a little more jam to the holes while the biscuits are
hot. Cool on wire racks. Makes 60.

muesli cookies

1/2 cup brown sugar
1/4 cup sugar
125g (4 oz) butter, softened
1 egg
1/2 cup malted milk powder
1 1/4 cups plain (all-purpose) flour, sifted
1/2 teaspoon bicarbonate of soda (baking soda)
3/4 cup rolled oats
1/4 cup dried apricots, chopped
1/4 cup dried apples, chopped
1/4 cup shredded coconut
1/4 cup sultanas
1 teaspoon cinnamon

Preheat the oven to 160°C (325°F). Place the sugars,
butter and egg in a bowl and beat with an electric mixer
until smooth. Add the milk powder, flour, bicarbonate of
soda, rolled oats, apricots, apples, coconut, sultanas and
cinnamon and mix until combined.
Roll 2 tablespoonfuls of the mixture into balls, place on
baking trays lined with non-stick baking paper and flatten
slightly. Bake for 18–20 minutes or until golden. Cool on
wire racks. Makes 14.

apricot oat slice

125g (4 oz) butter, melted
1/3 cup sugar
1 cup plain (all-purpose) flour
1/2 cup rolled oats
topping
2 eggs
1 cup brown sugar
1/3 cup plain (all-purpose) flour, sifted
1/2 teaspoon baking powder
200g (7 oz) chopped dried apricots
1 cup desiccated coconut

Preheat the oven to 180°C (350°F). Place the butter,
sugar, flour and rolled oats in a bowl and mix to combine.
Press the mixture into a 20cm x 30cm (8 in x 12 in) slice
tin lined with non-stick baking paper. Bake for 15 minutes
or until golden.
To make the topping, place the eggs and sugar in a bowl
and beat with electric beaters until light and fluffy.
Fold in the flour, baking powder, apricots and coconut.
Spread the topping over the base and bake for 20–25
minutes or until golden. Cool in the tin. Cut into slices.
Makes 24 slices.

chocolate brownie

200g (7 oz) dark couverture* chocolate, chopped
250g (8 oz) butter, chopped
1 3/4 cups brown sugar
4 eggs
1/3 cup cocoa powder, sifted
1 1/4 cups plain (all-purpose) flour, sifted
1/4 teaspoon baking powder

Preheat the oven to 160°C (325°F). Place the chocolate
and butter in a saucepan over low heat and stir until
smooth. Allow to cool slightly.
Place the sugar, eggs, cocoa, flour and baking powder in a
bowl. Add the chocolate mixture and mix until combined.
Pour the mixture into a 20cm (8 in) square slice tin lined
with non-stick baking paper. Bake for 50 minutes or until
set. Cool slightly in the tin. Cut into slices. Serve warm or
cold. Makes 16 slices.

jam drops

apricot oat slice

muesli cookies

chocolate brownie

melting moments

how to melting moments

175g (6 oz) butter, softened
¼ cup icing (confectioner's) sugar
1 teaspoon vanilla extract
1 cup plain (all-purpose) flour, sifted
¼ cup cornflour (cornstarch), sifted
filling
60g (2 oz) butter, softened
1 cup icing (confectioner's) sugar
2 teaspoons lemon juice
2 teaspoons finely grated lemon rind

Preheat the oven to 180°C (350°F). Place the butter, icing sugar and vanilla in a bowl and beat with electric beaters until light and fluffy. Stir in the flour and cornflour until combined.

Place the mixture into a piping bag fitted with a fluted nozzle. Pipe 3cm (1 in) rounds onto a baking tray lined with non-stick baking paper, allowing room for spreading. Cook for 12–14 minutes or until golden. Cool on trays.

To make the filling, place the butter, icing sugar, lemon juice and rind in a bowl and beat with electric beaters until fluffy and creamy. Pipe onto half the biscuits and sandwich with the remaining biscuits. Makes 16 filled biscuits.

Use these variations for different melting moment fillings.
orange **Replace the lemon juice and lemon rind in the filling with the same quantities of orange juice and rind.**
lime **Replace the lemon juice and lemon rind in the filling with the same quantities of lime juice and rind.**
chocolate **Omit the lemon juice and lemon rind. Use ¾ cup icing (confectioner's) sugar and ¼ cup cocoa powder for the filling and add 1 teaspoon vanilla extract and 1 teaspoon water.**
caramel **See the Short Order caramel filling on page 36.**

chocolate cheesecake brownie

vanilla slice

peanut cookies

chocolate cheesecake brownie

185g (6 oz) butter, melted
1/4 cup cocoa powder, sifted
1 cup caster (superfine) sugar
2 eggs
1 cup plain (all-purpose) flour, sifted
cheesecake
285g (9 1/2 oz) cream cheese, softened and chopped
4 1/2 tablespoons caster (superfine) sugar
2 eggs

Preheat the oven to 160°C (325°F). Place the butter, cocoa, sugar, eggs and flour in a bowl and mix well until smooth. Spoon into a 20cm (8 in) square slice tin lined with non-stick baking paper.
To make the cheesecake, process the cream cheese, sugar and eggs in a food processor until smooth.
Place large spoonfuls of the cheesecake mixture on top of the chocolate mixture and swirl with a butter knife. Bake for 45–50 minutes or until set. Cool in the tin. Cut into slices. Makes 16 slices.

vanilla slice

375g (13 oz) ready-prepared puff pastry
icing (confectioner's) sugar for dusting
vanilla cream
1 1/2 cups (12 fl oz) milk
1 1/2 cups (12 fl oz) (single or pouring) cream
60g (2 oz) butter
2 teaspoons vanilla extract
2/3 cup sugar
1/3 cup cornflour (cornstarch)
1/2 cup (4 fl oz) water
6 egg yolks

Preheat the oven to 180°C (350°F). Halve the pastry lengthwise and roll each piece out to a rectangle 2–3mm (1/8 in) thick. Trim each piece to fit a 20cm x 30cm (8 in x 12 in) slice tin. Place the pastry on baking trays lined with non-stick baking paper. Top each piece with another baking tray as a weight and bake for 35 minutes or until puffed and golden. Cool on racks.
To make the filling, place the milk, cream, butter, vanilla and sugar in a saucepan over medium-low heat and cook until hot but not boiling. Mix the cornflour and water to a smooth paste and whisk into the hot milk mixture. Add the egg yolks and stir, allowing to simmer, for 6 minutes or until the mixture has thickened. Remove from the heat and allow to cool to room temperature.
Place one of the pastry sheets in a 20cm x 30cm (8 in x 12 in) slice tin lined with non-stick baking paper. Spread over the filling and top with the remaining pastry. Refrigerate for 2 hours or until set. To serve, dust with icing sugar and slice. Makes 8 slices.

peanut cookies

125g (4 oz) butter
1/2 cup sugar
1 egg
1 1/4 cups plain (all-purpose) flour, sifted
1 teaspoon baking powder
150g (5 oz) raw peanuts

Preheat the oven to 180°C (350°F). Place the butter and sugar in the bowl of an electric mixer and beat until light and creamy. Add the egg and mix until combined. Fold through the flour, baking powder and peanuts.
Shape tablespoonfuls of the mixture into rounds. Place on baking trays lined with non-stick baking paper. Bake for 10–13 minutes or until golden. Cool on wire racks. Makes 28.

vanilla snap biscuits

185g (6 oz) butter
1 cup caster (superfine) sugar
1 1/2 teaspoons vanilla extract
2 1/2 cups plain (all-purpose) flour
1 egg
1 egg yolk, extra
icing (confectioner's) sugar to serve

Preheat the oven to 180°C (350°F). Process the butter, sugar and vanilla in a food processor until smooth. Add the flour, egg and egg yolk and process again to form a smooth dough. Knead the dough lightly, wrap in plastic wrap and refrigerate for 30 minutes.
Roll out the dough between sheets of non-stick baking paper until 5mm (1/4 in) thick. Cut the dough into shapes using cookie cutters. Place on baking trays lined with non-stick baking paper. Bake for 10–12 minutes or until golden. Cool on wire racks. To serve, dust with icing sugar. Makes 45.

Vanilla bean biscuits

vanilla and almond biscotti

how to vanilla + almond biscotti

2 cups plain (all-purpose) flour
1¹/2 teaspoons baking powder
³/4 cup sugar
³/4 cup blanched almonds
3 eggs
2¹/2 teaspoons vanilla extract

Preheat the oven to 160°C (325°F). Place the flour, baking powder, sugar and almonds in a bowl and mix together. Add the eggs and vanilla and mix well to form a dough. Divide the dough in two.

Place the dough on a lightly floured surface and knead each piece until smooth. Shape into logs and flatten slightly. Place the logs on a baking tray lined with non-stick baking paper and bake for 35 minutes. Remove from the oven and allow to cool completely.

Cut the logs into 5mm (¹/4 in) thick slices and place on a baking tray lined with non-stick baking paper. Bake for 10–15 minutes or until the biscotti are crisp. Store in an airtight container and serve dunked into espresso coffee or liqueur. Makes 40.

Try these biscotti flavour variations.
hazelnut and chocolate chip **Replace the almonds in the recipe above with ¹/2 cup roasted skinned hazelnuts and 40g (1¹/2 oz) chopped milk chocolate.**
double chocolate and hazelnut **Use 1³/4 cups plain (all-purpose) flour and ¹/4 cup cocoa powder instead of the flour in the recipe above. Use ¹/2 cup chopped dark chocolate and ¹/4 cup roasted skinned hazelnuts instead of the almonds.**
ginger and cinnamon **Replace the almonds in the recipe above with ³/4 cup chopped glacé ginger and add 1¹/2 teaspoons ground cinnamon.**

mixing tip **The mixture will be quite dry when you first combine the ingredients. You can start by mixing it to a dough in the bowl, then turn it out onto your work surface and continue working it by hand if necessary.**

baklava

36 sheets 20cm x 30cm (8 in x 12 in) filo pastry
125g (4 oz) butter, melted
3 tablespoons vegetable oil
filling
1¹/₂ cups chopped walnuts
1¹/₂ cups chopped blanched almonds
1 teaspoon ground cinnamon
¹/₃ cup brown sugar
45g (³/₄ oz) butter, softened
syrup
³/₄ cup (6 fl oz) water
1¹/₂ cups sugar

Preheat the oven to 160°C (325°F). To make the filling, process the walnuts, almonds, cinnamon, sugar and butter in a food processor until the nuts are finely chopped. Place a sheet of filo pastry in a 20cm x 30cm (8 in x 12 in) slice tin and brush with the combined melted butter and oil. Top with 11 more sheets of pastry, brushing each sheet with the butter and oil mixture.
Divide the nut filling in two and spread half over the pastry layers. Top with 12 more sheets of pastry, brushing each with the butter and oil mixture. Sprinkle evenly with the remaining filling and top with the remaining pastry, brushing each sheet with the remaining butter and oil. Cut the baklava into diamond shapes. Bake for 1 hour.
While the baklava is cooking, make the syrup. Place the water and sugar in a small saucepan over low heat and stir until the sugar is dissolved. Simmer for 6 minutes or until syrupy. Allow the hot baklava to stand for 5 minutes then pour over the syrup. Serve warm or cold. Makes 28 slices.

Greek almond cookies

250g (8 oz) butter, softened
³/₄ cup icing (confectioner's) sugar
1 teaspoon vanilla extract
2¹/₄ cups plain (all-purpose) flour
100g (3¹/₂ oz) chopped toasted almonds
icing (confectioner's) sugar to serve

Preheat the oven to 160°C (325°F). Place the butter, icing sugar and vanilla in a bowl and beat with electric beaters until light and creamy. Add the flour and almonds and mix to form a smooth dough. Refrigerate for 10 minutes or until the dough is firm.
Roll tablespoonfuls of the dough into a crescent shape and place on a baking tray lined with non-stick baking paper. Bake for 15 minutes or until golden. Cool on wire racks. To serve, sprinkle liberally with icing sugar. Makes 35.

panforte

1 cup blanched almonds
³/₄ cup hazelnuts
1 cup chopped dried apricots
1¹/₂ cups plain (all-purpose) flour, sifted
¹/₄ cup cocoa powder, sifted
1 teaspoon cinnamon
¹/₄ teaspoon allspice
1 cup (8 fl oz) honey
1 cup caster (superfine) sugar
rice paper* for lining

Preheat the oven to 180°C (350°F). Place the almonds and hazelnuts on separate baking trays and bake for 5 minutes or until golden. Set the almonds aside. Place the hazelnuts in a clean tea towel and rub to remove the skins. Roughly chop the almonds and hazelnuts.
Place the apricots, flour, cocoa, cinnamon and allspice in a large heatproof bowl.
Place the honey and sugar in a saucepan and stir over a low heat until the sugar is dissolved. Brush the sides of the pan with a pastry brush dipped in water to remove any sugar crystals. Increase the heat and allow the mixture to simmer for 1–2 minutes until 'soft ball' stage (113–115°C/235–240°F) (use a sugar or candy thermometer*). Pour into the flour mixture, add the almonds and hazelnuts and stir quickly to combine. Line a 20cm x 30cm (8 in x 12 in) slice tin with sheets of rice paper, trimming the edges to fit. Press the mixture into the tin. Cook for 20 minutes or until springy. Cool in the tin. Cut into slices. Makes 24 slices.

jam slice

125g (4 oz) butter, softened
¹/₃ cup caster (superfine) sugar
1 cup plain (all-purpose) flour, sifted
1 teaspoon baking powder
1 egg yolk
³/₄ cup raspberry jam (jelly)
topping
¹/₂ cup caster (superfine) sugar
1 egg, lightly beaten
1 cup desiccated coconut

Preheat the oven to 180°C (350°F). Process the butter, sugar, flour and baking powder in a food processor until combined. Add the egg yolk and continue to process until the mixture forms a soft dough. Press into a 20cm x 30cm (8 in x 12 in) slice tin lined with non-stick baking paper. Bake for 12–15 minutes or until the base is golden brown. Allow to cool then spread with the jam.
To make the topping, combine the sugar, egg and coconut. Sprinkle over the the jam. Bake for 25 minutes or until golden. Cool in the tin. Cut into slices. Makes 24 slices.

baklava

panforte

Greek almond cookies

jam slice

malted oat and raisin biscuits

double choc cookies

lemon slice

malted oat and raisin biscuits

1/2 cup brown sugar
1/4 cup sugar
125g (4 oz) butter, softened
1 egg
1/2 cup malted milk powder
1 1/4 cups plain (all-purpose) flour
1/4 teaspoon bicarbonate of soda (baking soda)
1/2 cup rolled oats
3/4 cup raisins

Preheat the oven to 160°C (325°F). Place the sugars, butter and egg in a bowl and beat with an electric mixer until light and creamy. Add the milk powder, flour, bicarbonate of soda, rolled oats and raisins and mix to combine.
Roll 2 tablespoonfuls of the mixture into flat rounds and place on baking trays lined with non-stick baking paper. Bake for 18–20 minutes or until golden. Cool on wire racks. Makes 15.

double choc cookies

250g (8 oz) butter, softened
1 cup brown sugar
3/4 cup sugar
3 eggs
2 1/4 cups plain (all-purpose) flour, sifted
1 teaspoon baking powder
1/2 cup cocoa powder
140g (4 1/2 oz) dark chocolate, broken into chunks
140g (4 1/2 oz) white chocolate, broken into chunks

Preheat the oven to 150°C (300°F). Place the butter and sugars in a bowl and beat until light and creamy. Add the eggs gradually and beat well. Add the flour, baking powder, cocoa and chocolate and mix well. Shape 2 tablespoonfuls of the mixture into rounds. Place on baking trays lined with non-stick baking paper, allowing room for the cookies to spread, and flatten slightly. Bake for 20–25 minutes or until dark brown on the bottom. Cool on wire racks. Makes 28.

lemon slice

1/2 cup caster (superfine) sugar
1 1/4 cups plain (all-purpose) flour
120g (4 oz) butter
1 tablespoon milk
topping
1 1/2 tablespoons cornflour (cornstarch)
2/3 cup (5 fl oz) (single or pouring) cream
6 eggs
1 3/4 cups caster (superfine) sugar
1 1/2 tablespoons finely grated lemon rind
3/4 cup (6 fl oz) lemon juice

Preheat the oven to 170°C (330°F). Process the sugar, flour, butter and milk in a food processor until the mixture comes together. Press into a 20cm x 30cm (8 in x 12 in) slice tin lined with non-stick baking paper. Bake for 25 minutes or until golden brown.
To make the topping, whisk together the cornflour and 2 tablespoons of the cream until a smooth paste forms. Whisk in the remaining cream, then the eggs, sugar, lemon rind and lemon juice. Place in a saucepan over low heat and cook, whisking, for 6 minutes or until the mixture thickens slightly. Pour over the base and bake for 5 minutes or until the topping is just set. Cool in the tin. Cut into slices. Makes 24 slices.

gingerbread men

125g (4 oz) butter, softened
1/2 cup brown sugar
1/2 cup golden syrup
2 1/2 cups plain (all-purpose) flour, sifted
2 teaspoons ground ginger
1 teaspoon bicarbonate of soda (baking soda)
icing
1 egg white ■
1/2 cup icing (confectioner's) sugar, sifted

Preheat the oven to 190°C (375°F). Place the butter and sugar in a bowl and beat with electric beaters until light and creamy. Add the golden syrup, flour, ginger and bicarbonate of soda and mix to form a smooth dough. Refrigerate for 10 minutes or until the dough is firm. Roll out the dough between sheets of non-stick baking paper to 4mm (1/4 in) thick. Cut out shapes from the dough using a gingerbread man cookie cutter. Place on baking trays lined with non-stick baking paper. Bake for 8–10 minutes or until golden brown. Cool on trays.
To make the icing, mix the egg white and icing sugar until combined. Pipe on buttons or spread over the cookies and allow to set. Makes 25.
■ If you don't want to use egg white, see page 36 for coloured icing for cookies.

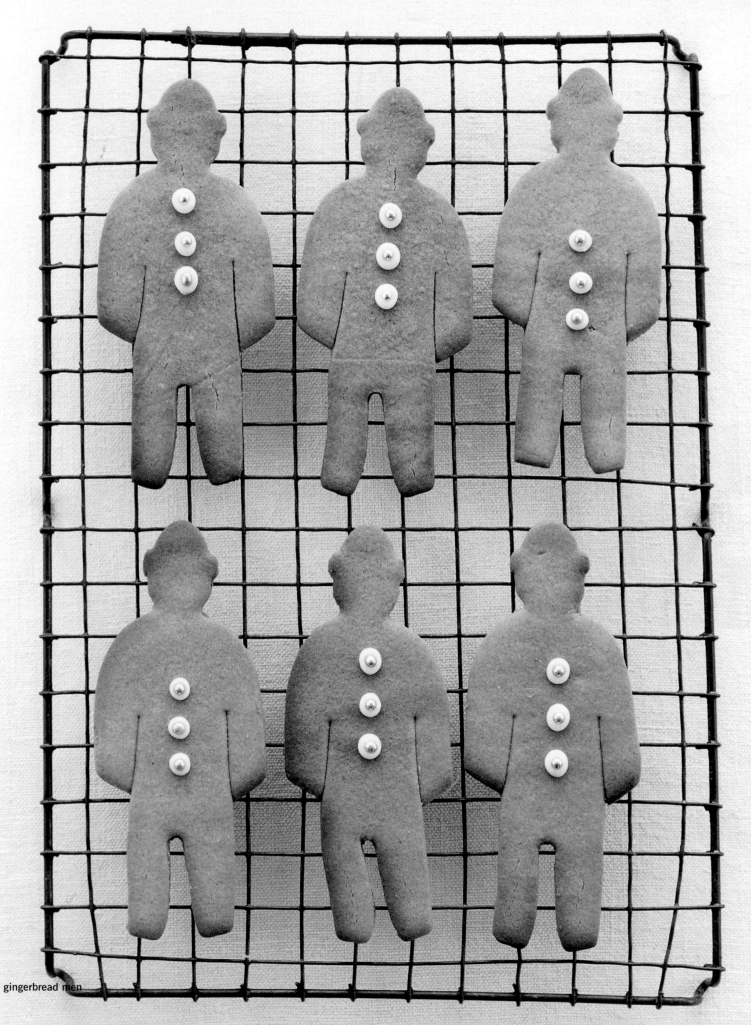

gingerbread men

short order

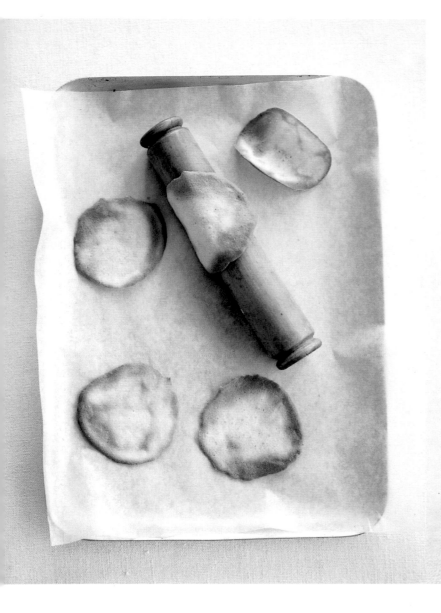

tuilles

coconut macaroons

coloured icing for cookies

short order

tuilles

Preheat the oven to 190°C (375°F). Whisk together 2 egg whites and 1/2 cup caster (superfine) sugar. Add 1/3 cup plain (all-purpose) flour, 1 teaspoon finely grated lemon rind, 1/2 teaspoon vanilla extract and 50g (11/2 oz) melted, cooled butter. Whisk until smooth. Place 2 teaspoonfuls of the mixture onto baking trays lined with non-stick baking paper and spread out to circles 8cm (31/4 in) in diameter, allowing room for spreading. Cook for 5–6 minutes or until just golden around the edges. While still hot, remove from the trays and place over a rolling pin to curl over the edges. Serve as a biscuit with dessert or coffee. Makes 16.

coconut macaroons

Preheat the oven to 180°C (350°F). Place 2 cups desiccated coconut, 1/2 cup caster (superfine) sugar and 2 egg whites in a bowl and mix to combine. Roll 2 teaspoonfuls of the mixture into balls, place on a baking tray lined with non-stick baking paper and flatten slightly. Cook for 10 minutes or until light golden. Makes 28.

coloured icing for cookies

Mix together 11/2 cups sifted pure icing (confectioner's) sugar and 2 tablespoons water until smooth. Add a couple of drops of food colouring and continue mixing until combined. Makes 2/3 cup.

ice-cream sandwiches

Preheat the oven to 180°C (350°F). Make a half quantity of the vanilla snap biscuits recipe (page 24). Roll out the dough between sheets of non-stick baking paper to 2mm (1/8 in) thick. Cut into 6mm (2 in) squares using a sharp knife or cookie cutter. Place on baking trays lined with non-stick baking paper. Bake for 10–12 minutes or until golden. (Alternatively, use readymade biscuits or cookies.) Sandwich readymade ice cream between the cookies. Roll the edges in grated dark chocolate. Makes 10.

chocolate ganache

Place 100g (31/2 oz) chopped dark couverture* chocolate and 1/2 cup (4 fl oz) (single or pouring) cream in a small saucepan over low heat. Stir until melted and glossy. Refrigerate until cool. Use as a filling for biscuits or as a rich icing over a slice or brownie. Makes 3/4 cup.

amaretti

Preheat the oven to 180°C (350°F). Process 200g (7 oz) raw almonds and 1 cup caster (superfine) sugar in a food processor until the almonds are roughly chopped. Add 1/4 cup plain (all-purpose) flour, 2 egg whites and 1 teaspoon vanilla extract and process until combined. Roll tablespoonfuls of the mixture into balls, place on a baking tray lined with non-stick baking paper and flatten slightly. Bake for 13 minutes or until light golden. Cool on trays. Serve with coffee. Makes 24.

caramel filling

Place 12/3 cups (13 fl oz) sweetened condensed milk, 100g (31/2 oz) butter and 2 tablespoons golden syrup in a saucepan over very low heat. Stir for 25–30 minutes or until thick and pale golden in colour. Allow to cool. Use to spread on biscuits or sandwich them together. Makes 13/4 cups.

peppermint filling

Sift 11/2 cups icing (confectioner's) sugar into a bowl. Gradually add 11/2 tablespoons water and 1/2 teaspoon peppermint essence and stir until combined. Use to spread on plain or chocolate biscuits or sandwich them together. Makes 2/3 cup.

ice-cream sandwiches

chocolate ganache

amaretti

caramel filling

peppermint filling

small cakes

dainty

delicate

nice

The small cake is *the must-have of the morning tea set.* There's something so very special about a lamington *perched on a pretty plate* with a cake fork, linen napkin and matching teacup on the side. Cupcakes, madeleines, friands and their other *sweetly petite* single-serve friends are also perfect for a lunchbox or picnic basket, road trip or party table. As an added bonus, there's no fighting over who gets the biggest piece.

The humble muffin, meanwhile, has revolutionised modern dining habits – *at last an excuse to eat cake for breakfast,* as well as mid-morning, at lunchtime, for afternoon tea or supper. And then there's the scone, the pancake and the pikelet, *reliable old favourites* you can whip up and cook in minutes, all waiting to team up with some jam and cream and to be *enjoyed whatever the occasion* or season.

blueberry muffins

how to blueberry muffins

2 cups plain (all-purpose) flour
2 teaspoons baking powder
3/4 cup caster (superfine) sugar
1 cup sour cream
2 eggs
1 teaspoon finely grated lemon rind
1/3 cup (2 1/2 fl oz) vegetable oil
1 1/4 cups fresh or frozen blueberries

Preheat the oven to 180°C (350°F). Sift the flour and baking powder into a bowl. Add the sugar and stir to combine.

Place the sour cream, eggs, lemon rind and oil in a bowl and whisk until smooth. Stir the sour cream mixture through the flour and sugar mixture until just combined.

Sprinkle over the blueberries and stir once. Spoon the mixture into 12 x 1/2 cup (4 fl oz) capacity non-stick muffin tins until two-thirds full. Bake for 12 minutes or until cooked when tested with a skewer. Makes 12.

For tender muffins that rise well, stir the mixture evenly and only until just combined. Do not overwork the mixture.
To make larger muffins, use 6 x 1 cup (8 fl oz) capacity muffin tins and bake them for 35 minutes.
raspberry and white chocolate muffins Omit the grated lemon rind. Replace the blueberries with 1 1/4 cups fresh or frozen raspberries and add 3/4 cup chopped white chocolate in step 3 above.
banana and cinnamon muffins Add 1 teaspoon ground cinnamon in step 1. Replace the blueberries with 1 cup chopped banana.

friands

orange and almond cake

espresso cakes

friands

125g (4 oz) butter
1 cup almond meal
1²/₃ cups icing (confectioner's) sugar, sifted
³/₄ cup plain (all-purpose) flour, sifted
¹/₂ teaspoon baking powder
5 egg whites
¹/₃ cup fresh or frozen raspberries, blueberries or
    sliced strawberries

Preheat the oven to 180°C (350°F). Place the butter in a saucepan over low heat and cook until melted and a very light golden colour. Set aside.
Place the almond meal, icing sugar, flour and baking powder in a bowl and stir to combine. Add the egg whites and stir to combine. Add the butter and stir to combine. Grease 10 x ¹/₂ cup (4 fl oz) capacity muffin tins. Spoon 2 tablespoons of the mixture into each tin and sprinkle the berries over the top. Bake for 15–20 minutes or until golden and springy to touch but moist in the centre. Makes 10.

orange and almond cakes

2 oranges, washed
65g (2 oz) butter, softened
1 cup caster (superfine) sugar
5 eggs
2¹/₂ cups almond meal
2 teaspoons baking powder
orange syrup
1 cup sugar
¹/₂ cup (4 fl oz) freshly squeezed orange juice
¹/₂ cup (4 fl oz) water

Place the oranges in a saucepan of water over medium heat. Cover and rapidly simmer for 1 hour or until very soft. Process the whole oranges in a food processor until very finely pureed.
Preheat the oven to 160°C (325°F). Place the butter and sugar in the bowl of an electric mixer and beat until light and creamy. Add the eggs gradually, beating well. Add the almond meal, baking powder and pureed orange and beat until smooth.
Grease and flour 6 x 1 cup (8 fl oz) capacity patty tins*. Spoon in the mixture and bake for 45 minutes or until cooked when tested with a skewer.
To make the orange syrup, place the sugar, orange juice and water in a saucepan over medium heat. Boil for 10–15 minutes or until syrupy. To serve, spoon the syrup over the warm cakes. Serve with thick (double) cream. Makes 6.

espresso cakes

100g (3¹/₂ oz) butter, very well softened
1 cup caster (superfine) sugar
3 eggs
1¹/₄ cups plain (all-purpose) flour, sifted
2 teaspoons baking powder, sifted
¹/₄ cup hazelnut meal*
1¹/₂ tablespoons instant coffee granules or powder
    dissolved in 1 tablespoon boiling water

Preheat the oven to 160°C (325°F). Place the butter, sugar, eggs, flour, baking powder, hazelnut meal and coffee mixture in a bowl. Combine using electric beaters on low speed, then increase to high speed and mix until just smooth.
Grease 10 x ¹/₂ cup (4 fl oz) capacity muffin or patty tins*. Spoon in the mixture and bake for 25 minutes or until cooked when tested with a skewer. Cool in the tins for 10 minutes then remove and cool on a rack. Pour over chocolate glaze (page 96) and serve with strong coffee. Makes 10.

profiteroles

1 cup (8 fl oz) water
100g (3¹/₂ oz) butter, chopped
³/₄ cup plain (all-purpose) flour, sifted
4 eggs
melted dark chocolate for topping

Preheat the oven to 200°C (400°F). Place the water and butter in a saucepan over low heat and cook until the butter is melted and the mixture starts to simmer. Add the flour and beat with a wooden spoon until smooth. Cook, stirring, over low heat until the mixture leaves the side of the pan. Remove from the heat and gradually beat in the eggs.
Place the mixture into a piping bag. Pipe or drop 3 teaspoons of the mixture onto baking trays lined with non-stick baking paper. Bake for 30 minutes or until light golden. Turn off the oven, keep the door slightly open using a wooden spoon and leave the profiteroles in the oven for 15 minutes or until golden and hollow-sounding when tapped. Cool on wire racks.
Place a creamy filling of your choice, such as whipped cream, crème pâtissière (page 174) or chocolate mousse (page 106) in a piping bag. Push the nozzle through the base of the profiterole and squeeze in enough mixture to fill it.
To finish, dip the top of each profiterole in melted chocolate or hot toffee (use the crème caramel base recipe, page 111) and allow to set. Makes 30.

profiteroles

mango and coconut cakes

125g (4 oz) butter
1 cup almond meal
1²/3 cups icing (confectioner's) sugar, sifted
³/4 cup plain (all-purpose) flour, sifted
¹/2 teaspoon baking powder, sifted
5 egg whites
160g (5¹/2 oz) fresh or frozen mango cheek, finely chopped
meringue icing
1¹/2 cups sugar
¹/2 cup (4 fl oz) water
3 egg whites

Preheat the oven to 180°C (350°F). Place the butter in a saucepan over low heat and cook until melted and a very light golden colour. Set aside.
Place the almond meal, icing sugar, flour and baking powder in a bowl and stir to combine. Add the egg whites, then the butter, then the mango, stirring to combine between each addition.
Grease 8 x ¹/2 cup (4 fl oz) capacity tins. Spoon in the mixture and bake for 20 minutes or until golden and springy to touch but moist in the centre. Cool on wire racks. To make the meringue icing, place the sugar and water in a saucepan over low heat and stir until the sugar is dissolved. Boil for 7–8 minutes or until the mixture reaches 'soft ball' stage (116°C/240°F on a sugar or candy thermometer*). Beat the egg whites with an electric mixer until foamy. Add the sugar syrup in a slow stream and continue beating until the mixture is thick and glossy. Spread over the cakes immediately. Makes 8.

flourless chocolate cakes

180g (6 oz) butter, chopped
220g (7¹/2 oz) quality dark cooking chocolate, chopped
1¹/4 cups caster (superfine) sugar
³/4 cup almond meal
1 cup cocoa powder, sifted
5 eggs

Preheat the oven to 140°C (280°F). Place the butter, chocolate and sugar in a saucepan over low heat and stir until melted and smooth. Place the almond meal and cocoa in a bowl and whisk in the chocolate mixture. Add the eggs gradually, whisking until well combined. Grease 12 x ¹/2 cup (4 fl oz) capacity non-stick muffin tins. Spoon in the mixture and bake for 30 minutes or until firm. Allow to cool in the tins. Serve with thick (double) cream or chocolate glaze (page 96) and fresh berries if desired. Makes 12.

little apricot tea cakes

125g (4 oz) butter, softened
1 cup caster (superfine) sugar
1 teaspoon vanilla extract
2 eggs
1¹/2 cups plain (all-purpose) flour
1¹/2 teaspoons baking powder
6 apricots, stoned and thinly sliced
2 teaspoons icing (confectioner's) sugar

Preheat the oven to 160°C (325°F). Place the butter, sugar and vanilla in the bowl of an electric mixer and beat until light and creamy. Add the eggs gradually and beat well. Sift over the flour and baking powder and stir to combine.
Spoon the mixture into 12 x ¹/2 cup (4 fl oz) capacity muffin tins lined with paper patty cases. Place the apricot slices on top of the mixture and dust with icing sugar. Bake for 25 minutes or until cooked when tested with a skewer. Remove from the tins and serve in the patty cases. Makes 12.

meringues

4 egg whites (150ml/5 fl oz) ▪
1 cup caster (superfine) sugar
2 teaspoons cornflour (cornstarch)
1 teaspoon white vinegar

Preheat the oven to 150°C (300°F). Place the egg whites in the bowl of an electric mixer and beat until soft peaks form. Gradually add the sugar and beat until glossy. Sift the cornflour over the mixture and fold through with the vinegar.
Place ¹/3 cup portions of the mixture on baking trays lined with non-stick baking paper and shape into small rounds. Place in the oven, reduce the heat to 120°C (250°F) and bake for 30–35 minutes. Turn the oven off and allow the meringues to cool while still in the oven. Makes 12.
▪ Measure the egg whites accurately for perfect meringues.

mango and coconut cakes

little apricot tea cakes

flourless chocolate cakes

meringues

how to hot cross buns

1 tablespoon active dry yeast
1/2 cup caster (superfine) sugar
1 1/2 cups (12 fl oz) lukewarm milk
4 1/4 cups plain (all-purpose) flour, sifted
2 teaspoons mixed spice
2 teaspoons ground cinnamon
50g (1 1/2 oz) butter, melted
1 egg
1 1/2 cups sultanas
1/3 cup candied mixed peel, optional
1/2 cup plain (all-purpose) flour, extra
1/3 cup (2 1/2 fl oz) water
1 quantity glaze (page 174)

Place the yeast, 2 teaspoons of the sugar and all of the milk in a bowl and set aside for 5 minutes. The mixture will start to foam, indicating that the yeast is active.

Add the flour, mixed spice, cinnamon, butter, egg, sultanas, mixed peel and remaining sugar to the yeast mixture and mix using a butter knife until a sticky dough forms. Knead the dough on a lightly floured surface for 8 minutes or until it feels elastic. Place in an oiled bowl, cover with a tea towel and allow to stand in a warm place for 1 hour or until doubled in size. Divide the dough into 12 pieces and roll into balls.

Grease a 23cm (9 in) square cake tin and line with non-stick baking paper. Place the dough balls in the tin, cover with a clean tea towel and set aside in a warm place for 30 minutes or until they rise. Preheat the oven to 200°C (400°F). Combine the extra flour and water, place in a piping bag or a plastic bag with one corner snipped off, and pipe crosses on the buns. Bake for 35 minutes or until well browned and springy to touch. Brush with the warm glaze while the buns are hot. Serve warm with butter. Makes 12.

hot cross buns

banana cinnamon bread

cupcakes with crushed raspberry cream

madeleines

banana cinnamon breads

140g (5 oz) butter
1/2 cup caster (superfine) sugar
1 egg
1 1/2 cups plain (all-purpose) flour, sifted
3/4 teaspoon baking powder, sifted
1/2 cup hazelnut meal*
1/3 cup (2 1/2 fl oz) buttermilk
1/2 teaspoon ground cinnamon
1 large or 2 small bananas, sliced
melted butter for brushing
demerara sugar* for sprinkling

Preheat the oven to 180°C (350°F). Place the butter and sugar in the bowl of an electric mixer and beat until light and creamy. Add the egg and beat well. Add the flour, baking powder, hazelnut meal, buttermilk and cinnamon and fold through until smooth.
Grease 6 x 3/4 cup (6 fl oz) capacity tins. Spoon in the mixture and place the banana slices on top. Brush with the melted butter, sprinkle with the demerara sugar and bake for 35 minutes or until golden and cooked when tested with a skewer. Serve warm or cold. Makes 6.

cupcakes with crushed raspberry cream

125g (4 oz) butter, softened
3 eggs
1 1/2 cups plain (all-purpose) flour
1 1/2 teaspoons baking powder
2/3 cup caster (superfine) sugar
1/4 cup (2 fl oz) milk
1 teaspoon vanilla extract
crushed raspberry cream
250g (8 oz) raspberries
1 cup thick (double) cream
1 tablespoon icing (confectioner's) sugar, sifted

Preheat the oven to 180°C (350°F). Place the butter, eggs, flour, baking powder, sugar, milk and vanilla in the bowl of an electric mixer and beat for 4 minutes or until smooth and a pale creamy colour.
Line 12 x 1/2 cup (4 fl oz) capacity patty tins* with deep paper patty cases. Spoon in the mixture to three-quarters full. Bake for 18–20 minutes or until cooked when tested with a skewer. Cool on wire racks.
To make the crushed raspberry cream, place the raspberries in a bowl and crush lightly with a fork. Add the cream and icing sugar and fold to combine.
To serve, use a teaspoon to scoop out a hole in the top of each cake, reserving the scooped-out pieces. Fill the holes with the crushed raspberry cream and replace the cake pieces. Makes 12.

madeleines

4 eggs
3/4 cup caster (superfine) sugar
1 1/4 cups plain (all-purpose) flour
2 teaspoons baking powder
180g (6 oz) butter, melted and cooled

Preheat the oven to 180°C (350°F). Place the eggs and sugar in the bowl of an electric mixer and beat for 8–10 minutes or until very pale and thick. Sift the flour and baking powder over the mixture and continue to beat at low speed until smooth. Add the butter and beat until combined.
Grease two madeleine tins* with 12 x 1 1/2 tablespoon capacity holes. Spoon in the mixture and bake for 8–10 minutes or until risen and golden. Makes 24.

lemon cakes with passionfruit syrup

175g (6 oz) butter, very well softened
3/4 cup caster (superfine) sugar
1 tablespoon finely grated lemon rind
3 eggs
1 1/2 cups plain (all-purpose) flour
2 teaspoons baking powder
2 teaspoons lemon juice
passionfruit syrup
1 cup caster (superfine) sugar
1 cup (8 fl oz) water
2/3 cup passionfruit pulp (about 6 passionfruit)

Preheat the oven to 160°C (325°F). Place the butter, sugar and lemon rind in the bowl of an electric mixer and beat until light and creamy. Gradually add the eggs and beat well. Sift the flour and baking powder over the mixture and fold through with the lemon juice.
Grease 12 x 1/2 cup (4 fl oz) capacity muffin tins. Spoon in the mixture and bake for 25 minutes or until cooked when tested with a skewer.
While the cakes are cooking, make the passionfruit syrup. Place the sugar, water and passionfruit pulp in a saucepan over low heat and stir until the sugar is dissolved. Increase the heat and allow the mixture to boil for 6–8 minutes or until syrupy.
To serve, spoon the hot syrup over the hot cakes. Makes 12.

lemon cake with passionfruit syrup

brioche

1½ teaspoons active dry yeast
1 teaspoon sugar
¼ cup (2 fl oz) lukewarm milk
1 cup plain (all-purpose) flour, sifted
1 tablespoon sugar, extra
1 egg
90g (3 oz) butter, softened

Place the yeast, sugar and milk in a bowl and set aside for
5 minutes. The mixture will start to foam, indicating that
the yeast is active.
Process the yeast mixture, flour, extra sugar and egg in
a food processor until combined. With the motor still
running, add the butter a little at a time and process
until a very soft and sticky dough forms. Place in a greased
bowl, cover with plastic wrap and set aside in a warm place
for 30 minutes or until the dough has doubled in size.
Preheat the oven to 190°C (375°F). Grease 6 x ½ cup
(4 fl oz) capacity moulds. Divide the dough between the
moulds and smooth over the tops. Set aside for 20 minutes
to rise again. Bake for 15 minutes or until golden. Remove
from the moulds and serve warm or cold. Serve plain or
with candied citrus peel and syrup (page 96).

pancakes

2 cups plain (all-purpose) flour, sifted
3 teaspoons baking powder, sifted
½ cup caster (superfine) sugar
1 egg
1¼ cups (10 fl oz) milk
¾ cup (6 fl oz) buttermilk
75g (2½ oz) butter, melted

Place the flour, baking powder and sugar in a bowl. Place
the egg, milk, buttermilk and butter in a separate bowl and
whisk until combined. Add the milk mixture to the flour
mixture and whisk until smooth.
Heat a non-stick frying pan over medium–low heat. Pour
⅓ cup (2½ fl oz) of the mixture at a time into the pan
and cook until bubbles appear on the surface. Turn the
pancake and cook for 1 minute or until golden. Keep the
pancakes warm while cooking the remaining mixture.
Serve in small stacks with maple syrup, lemon and sugar,
butter or fresh fruit. Makes 15.

brioche

pancakes

how to doughnuts

4 teaspoons active dry yeast
1/4 cup (2 fl oz) lukewarm water
1 cup (8 fl oz) lukewarm milk
3 tablespoons caster (superfine) sugar
100g (3 1/2 oz) butter, melted
4 1/4 cups plain (all-purpose) flour
3 eggs
vegetable oil for deep-frying
1 cup caster (superfine) sugar, extra
1 teaspoon ground cinnamon

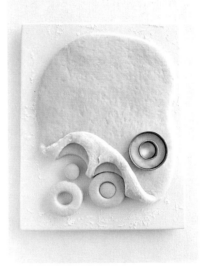

Place the yeast, water, milk and 1 tablespoon of the sugar in a bowl and set aside for 10 minutes. The mixture will start to foam, indicating that the yeast is active.

Add the butter, flour, eggs and remaining sugar to the yeast mixture and mix with a butter knife until a sticky dough forms. Bring the dough together by kneading on a lightly floured surface. Place the dough in an oiled bowl, cover with a tea towel and set aside in a warm place for 45 minutes or until doubled in size.
Knead the dough on a lightly floured surface for 5 minutes or until it feels smooth and elastic when pressed.

Roll out the dough on a lightly floured surface until 1cm (1/2 in) thick. Cut 8cm (3 1/4 in) rounds with a cutter. Cut a 3.5cm (1 1/4 in) hole in the middle of the rounds. ∎ Place on a tray lined with non-stick baking paper, cover with a tea towel and set aside in a warm place for 30 minutes or until risen. Heat the oil in a saucepan over medium–low heat. Cook the doughnuts a few at a time for 1 minute each side or until golden. Drain briefly on paper towel and toss in the combined sugar and cinnamon. Makes 30.

For jam doughnuts, see page 62.
∎ After cutting out the doughnut shapes, gather together the dough scraps, knead them together and roll out again to make more doughnuts.

doughnuts

short order

scones

jam doughnut

lamingtons

short order

scones

Preheat the oven to 180°C (350°F). Whisk 2½ cups (20 fl oz) (single or pouring) cream until soft peaks form. Sift over 3 cups plain (all-purpose) flour and 3 teaspoons baking powder. Add 2 tablespoons caster (superfine) sugar and stir to combine. Turn onto a lightly floured surface and press out the dough until 3cm (1 in) thick. Cut into 4cm (1½ in) rounds, place on a baking tray lined with non-stick baking paper and brush the tops with a little milk. Bake for 12–15 minutes or until the scones are puffed and golden. Serve warm with jam (jelly) and cream. Makes 12.

jam doughnuts

Follow the doughnut recipe on page 58 but do not cut out the middle holes. Cook until golden, drain on paper towel, then pierce each doughnut with the tip of a knife and pipe in a little raspberry or strawberry jam (jelly). Toss in sugar and serve. Or fill with crème pâtissière (page 174) for custard doughnuts. Makes 22.

lamingtons

Make 1 quantity sponge cake (page 75) in an 18cm (7 in) square cake tin and cool on a wire rack. Cut into 6cm (2½ in) squares. Sift together 3 cups icing (confectioner's) sugar and ¾ cup cocoa powder, and mix with ⅓ cup (2½ fl oz) boiling water and 75g (2½ oz) melted butter. Toss the sponge squares in the chocolate icing and then in desiccated coconut. Allow to set on a wire rack. Makes 9.

almond cakes with sugared raspberries

Follow the friand recipe on page 46 and pour the mixture into 6 x 1 cup (8 fl oz) capacity muffin tins. Bake for 25 minutes or until cooked when tested with a skewer. Cool and drizzle with basic icing (this page). Brush some raspberries with a little egg white, toss in caster (superfine) sugar and place on top of the cakes. Makes 6.

peanut butter cupcakes

Preheat the oven to 160°C (325°F). Place 175g (6 oz) very soft butter, ¾ cup caster (superfine) sugar, 3 eggs, 1¾ cups sifted plain (all-purpose) flour and 2 teaspoons baking powder in a bowl and mix using electric beaters until just smooth. Line 12 x ½ cup (4 fl oz) patty tins* with paper patty cases. Spoon in the mixture and swirl 1½ teaspoons peanut butter through each cake. Bake for 20 minutes. Makes 12.

basic icing

Sift 1½ cups icing (confectioner's) sugar into a bowl. Mix through 2 tablespoons water or 2 tablespoons lemon juice and 1 teaspoon grated lemon rind or 2 tablespoons orange juice and 1 teaspoon grated orange rind until smooth. Makes ¾ cup.

pikelets

Combine 2 cups plain (all-purpose) flour, 2 teaspoons baking powder and ½ cup caster (superfine) sugar in a bowl. Combine 2 eggs, 1½ cups (12 fl oz) milk and 70g (2 oz) melted butter in another bowl, then whisk into the flour mixture. Cook 1 tablespoon of the mixture over low heat in a frying pan greased with butter for 1–2 minutes. Turn and cook for 1 minute or until golden. Serve the pikelets warm with lemon and sugar or cool with jam (jelly) and whipped cream. Makes 40.

maple syrup cakes

Preheat the oven to 180°C (350°F). Beat 90g (3 oz) softened butter, ⅔ cup brown sugar and 2½ tablespoons caster (superfine) sugar in the bowl of an electric mixer until light and creamy. Add 2 eggs gradually and beat well. Add 2 tablespoons milk, ½ cup maple syrup, 1⅔ cups sifted plain (all-purpose) flour and 1¾ teaspoons baking powder and beat until just smooth. Spoon into 12 x ½ cup (4 fl oz) capacity muffin tins and bake for 20 minutes or until cooked when tested with a skewer. Cool in the tins for 5 minutes. Transfer to a rack. Makes 12.

almond cakes with
sugared raspberries

peanut butter cupcakes

basic lemon or orange icing

pikelets

maple syrup cakes

cakes

indulgent

luscious

delectable

Favourite cakes have a *special place in our hearts* just like the people who make them. My grandmother was known for her *rich and tasty* fruit cake, endless slices of which appeared from an old metal biscuit tin she kept in her pantry. One of my aunts is famous for her freshly baked *light-as-air sponge cakes,* always *generously filled* with homemade jam and whipped cream. A dear friend of mine bakes a legendary cheesecake that everyone begs her to bring to birthdays, parties, anything. *What a great way to win friends,* influence people and always be thought of in a warm and loving way.

Favourite cakes also have a special place in our memories. I can't remember the gifts I received for my sixth birthday, but I can still picture and almost taste the butter cake my mother made, with its pink icing, hundreds and thousands and silver cachous. *That's the real magic of cakes.*

butter cake

how to butter cake

125g (4 oz) butter, very well softened
1 teaspoon vanilla extract
1 cup caster (superfine) sugar
3 eggs
1 1/2 cups plain (all-purpose) flour, sifted
1/2 teaspoon baking powder, sifted
1/4 teaspoon bicarbonate of
   soda (baking soda), sifted
1/2 cup (4 fl oz) milk

Preheat the oven to 150°C (300°F). Place the butter, vanilla, sugar, eggs, flour, baking powder, bicarbonate of soda and milk in the bowl of an electric mixer and beat on a low speed until combined.

Increase the speed to high and beat the mixture until it is just smooth.

Grease a 20cm (8 in) round cake tin and line with non-stick baking paper. Spoon in the mixture and bake for 1 hour 5 minutes or until cooked when tested with a skewer. Allow to cool for 5 minutes then turn onto a wire rack. Serve plain or spread with basic icing (page 62). Serves 8.

coffee butter cake **Dissolve 2 tablespoons instant coffee granules or powder in 1 tablespoon boiling water and add in step 1 above before mixing.**
orange butter cake **Add 1 tablespoon finely grated orange rind in step 1 above before mixing.**
lemon butter cake **Add 1 tablespoon finely grated lemon rind in step 1 above before mixing.**
spiced butter cake **Add 1 teaspoon either cinnamon or mixed spice in step 1 above before mixing.**

madeira cake

muddy chocolate cake

orange and poppyseed cake

madeira cake

170g (5¹/2 oz) butter, softened
3/4 cup caster (superfine) sugar
1 tablespoon finely grated lemon rind
3 eggs
1¹/2 tablespoons lemon juice
3/4 cup plain (all-purpose) flour
3/4 teaspoon baking powder
2/3 cup almond meal

Preheat the oven to 170°C (330°F). Place the butter, sugar and lemon rind in the bowl of an electric mixer and beat until light and creamy. Gradually add the eggs and the lemon juice, beating well. Sift the flour and baking powder over the butter mixture and fold through with the almond meal.
Grease a 10cm x 20cm (4 in x 8 in) loaf tin and line the base with non-stick baking paper. Spoon in the mixture and bake for 45 minutes or until cooked when tested with a skewer. Cool in the tin for 5 minutes then turn onto a wire rack. Serves 8–10.

muddy chocolate cake

300g (10 oz) dark couverture chocolate*, chopped
250g (8 oz) butter
5 eggs, separated
1/3 cup caster (superfine) sugar
1 teaspoon vanilla extract
1/3 cup plain (all-purpose) flour
1/2 teaspoon baking powder

Preheat the oven to 130°C (260°F). Place the chocolate and butter in a saucepan over low heat and stir until melted and smooth. Set aside.
Place the egg yolks, sugar and vanilla in the bowl of an electric mixer and beat until thick and pale.
Place the egg whites in a separate bowl and beat until stiff peaks form.
Fold the chocolate mixture through the egg yolk mixture. Sift over the flour and baking powder and gently fold through. Carefully fold the egg whites through. Pour the mixture into a 20cm (8 in) round cake tin lined with non-stick baking paper. Bake for 1 hour 15 minutes or until the cake is firm. Cool in the tin. Spread the cooled cake with chocolate glaze (page 96) and serve at room temperature■ with thick (double) cream and berries if desired. Serves 8–10.
■ For the best flavour and texture, serve this cake at room temperature, not chilled.

orange and poppyseed cake

1/3 cup poppy seeds
3/4 cup (6 fl oz) milk
200g (7 oz) butter, softened
1 tablespoon finely grated orange rind
3/4 cup caster (superfine) sugar
3 eggs
2 cups plain (all-purpose) flour
1¹/2 teaspoons baking powder
1/2 cup (4 fl oz) freshly squeezed orange juice
syrup
1 cup sugar
1 cup (8 fl oz) freshly squeezed orange juice
1/2 cup shredded orange rind

Preheat the oven to 160°C (325°F). Place the poppy seeds and milk in a bowl and stir to combine. Set aside.
Place the butter, orange rind and sugar in the bowl of an electric mixer and beat until light and creamy. Gradually add the eggs and beat well. Sift the flour and baking powder over the butter mixture and add the orange juice and poppy seed and milk mixture. Stir to combine and spoon into a 20cm (8 in) round cake tin lined with non-stick baking paper. Bake for 55–60 minutes or until cooked when tested with a skewer.
While the cake is cooking, make the syrup. Place the sugar, orange juice and orange rind in a saucepan over low heat and stir until the sugar is dissolved. Increase the heat and boil for 5–6 minutes or until syrupy.
Pour half of the hot syrup over the hot cake. To serve, cut the warm or cold cake into wedges and pour over the remaining syrup. Serves 8–10.

melt-and-mix white chocolate cake

185g (6 oz) butter, chopped
1 cup (8 fl oz) milk
1¹/2 cups caster (superfine) sugar
150g (5 oz) white chocolate, chopped
2 cups plain (all-purpose) flour, sifted
1¹/2 teaspoons baking powder
1 teaspoon vanilla extract
2 eggs

Preheat the oven to 160°C (325°F). Place the butter, milk, sugar and chocolate in a saucepan over low heat and stir until melted and smooth.
Place the flour, baking powder, vanilla and eggs in a bowl. Add the chocolate mixture and whisk until smooth. Pour the mixture into a 22cm (9 in) round cake tin lined with non-stick baking paper. Bake for 50 minutes or until cooked when tested with a skewer. Cool in the tin. Spread the cooled cake with chocolate glaze (page 96). Serves 8–10.

melt-and-mix white chocolate cake

sponge cake

how to sponge cake

1¹/4 cups plain (all-purpose) flour
6 eggs
³/4 cup caster (superfine) sugar
60g (2 oz) butter, melted

Preheat the oven to 180°C (350°F). Sift the flour three times. Set aside. Place the eggs and sugar in the bowl of an electric mixer and beat for 8–10 minutes or until thick and pale and tripled in volume.

Sift the flour over the egg and sugar mixture and gently fold through. Fold through the butter. Grease two shallow 20cm (8 in) ▪ round cake tins and line the bases with non-stick baking paper.

Pour half the mixture into each tin and bake for 25 minutes or until the cakes are springy to touch and come away from the sides of the tin. Cool on wire racks. Fill with whipped cream and jam (jelly) of your choice. To serve, sprinkle with extra caster sugar. Serves 8–10.

For a light and airy sponge, use a metal spoon to fold the flour through the egg mixture with a gentle cutting, lifting and folding action.
The following fillings are great variations on the traditional jam and cream.
lemon curd filling Use lemon curd (page 124) instead of jam (jelly) with the cream to fill the sponge.
fruit filling Fill the cooled sponge with cream and your choice of raspberries, blueberries or thinly sliced strawberries, peaches or apricots.
▪ This recipe can also be used to make one deep 18cm (7 in) square sponge cake.

marble cake

250g (8 oz) butter, softened
1¼ cups caster (superfine) sugar
1 teaspoon vanilla extract
4 eggs
2¼ cups plain (all-purpose) flour
2¼ teaspoons baking powder
1 cup (8 fl oz) milk
pink food colouring
¼ cup cocoa powder, sifted
2 tablespoons caster (superfine) sugar, extra
1 tablespoon milk, extra

Preheat the oven to 160°C (325°F). Place the butter, sugar and vanilla in the bowl of an electric mixer and beat until light and creamy. Gradually add the eggs and beat well. Sift the flour and baking powder over the butter mixture and fold through with the milk. Divide the mixture into three. Colour one portion with pink colouring. Stir the cocoa and extra sugar and milk through another. Grease a 25cm (10 in) fluted (bundt) cake tin*. Drop alternate spoonfuls of pink, chocolate and plain cake mixture into the tin. Swirl a butter knife through the mixture to give a marbled effect. Bake for 50–55 minutes or until cooked when tested with a skewer. Cool on a wire rack. Spread with basic icing (page 62) or meringue icing (mango and coconut cakes, page 48). Serves 8–10.

simple lemon cake

220g (7½ oz) butter, melted
1½ cups caster (superfine) sugar
2 eggs
1 cup sour cream
¼ cup (2 fl oz) lemon juice
2 tablespoons finely grated lemon rind
2 cups plain (all-purpose) flour
2 teaspoons baking powder

Preheat the oven to 180°C (350°F). Place the butter, sugar, eggs, sour cream, lemon juice and lemon rind in the bowl of an electric mixer and mix on low speed until combined. Sift the flour and baking powder over the mixture and beat on medium speed for 3–4 minutes or until smooth. Spoon the mixture into a shallow 20cm x 30cm (8 in x 12 in) cake tin lined with non-stick baking paper and bake for 35 minutes or until golden and cooked through when tested with a skewer. Serve the cake warm or allow to cool completely and spread with basic icing (page 62). Serves 12.

apple and cinnamon tea cake

185g (6 oz) butter, softened
½ teaspoon ground cinnamon
⅔ cup caster (superfine) sugar
3 eggs
1½ cups plain (all-purpose) flour
½ teaspoon baking powder
⅓ cup (2½ fl oz) milk
topping
4 small green apples, peeled, halved and cored
1 teaspoon sugar
¼ teaspoon ground cinnamon
¼ cup apricot jam (jelly), warmed

Preheat the oven to 160°C (325°F). Place the butter, cinnamon and sugar in the bowl of an electric mixer and beat until light and creamy. Gradually add the eggs and beat well. Sift the flour and baking powder over the butter mixture, add the milk and stir until combined. Line the base of a 22cm (9 in) springform tin* with non-stick baking paper and spoon in the mixture.
To make the topping, cut a row of deep slits in each apple half and arrange over the top of the cake mixture. Combine the sugar and cinnamon and sprinkle over the apples. Bake for 50 minutes. Brush the cake with the warm jam and return to the oven for 10 minutes or until cooked when tested with a skewer. Serve warm with thick (double) cream. Serves 8–10.

caramel layer cake

1¼ cups plain (all-purpose) flour
6 eggs
3½ tablespoons caster (superfine) sugar
3½ tablespoons brown sugar
125g (4 oz) butter, melted
2 cups thick (double) cream
caramel sauce (page 96), completely cooled

Preheat the oven to 180°C (350°F). Sift the flour three times and set aside.
Place the eggs, caster sugar and brown sugar in the bowl of an electric mixer and beat for 8–10 minutes or until pale and thick and tripled in volume. Sift the flour over the mixture and fold gently to combine. Fold in the butter. Grease an 18cm (7 in) square cake tin and line the base with non-stick baking paper. Spoon in the mixture and bake for 25 minutes or until the cake comes away from the side of the tin. Cool in the tin for 5 minutes then turn out onto a wire rack. When completely cool, slice the cake in half. To serve ■, spread one half of the cake with half the cream and caramel. Top with the other half of cake and spread with the remaining cream and caramel. Serves 8–10.
■ This cake is best eaten on the day it is made.

marble cake

apple and cinnamon tea cake

simple lemon cake

caramel layer cake

grandma's fruit cake

banana cake

sour cream pound cake

grandma's fruit cake

3 cups raisins
1¼ cups sultanas
¾ cup currants
⅔ cup candied mixed peel
1 cup slivered almonds
¾ cup chopped dates
¾ cup (6 fl oz) brandy or sherry
250g (8 oz) butter, softened
1¼ cups brown sugar
4 eggs
2¼ cups plain (all-purpose) flour, sifted
¼ teaspoon bicarbonate of soda (baking soda)
1 teaspoon ground cinnamon
½ teaspoon ground allspice
2–3 tablespoons brandy or sherry, extra

Place the raisins, sultanas, currants, mixed peel, almonds
and dates in a bowl and pour over the brandy. Cover and
allow to macerate for at least 8 hours or overnight.
Preheat the oven to 140°C (280°F). Place the butter and
sugar in the bowl of an electric mixer and beat until light
and creamy. Gradually add the eggs and beat well. Place
the butter mixture, soaked fruit mixture, flour, bicarbonate
of soda, cinnamon and allspice in a large bowl and stir to
combine. Line a 20cm (8 in) square cake tin with two
layers of non-stick baking paper. Spoon in the mixture
and bake for 2 hours or until cooked when tested with a
skewer. Pour over the extra brandy or sherry while the cake
is still hot. Cool in the tin. This cake may be stored in an
airtight container for up to 2 months. Serves 12.

banana cake

125g (4 oz) butter, softened
1 cup caster (superfine) sugar
¼ cup brown sugar
3 eggs
2 cups plain (all-purpose) flour
2 teaspoons baking powder
1 teaspoon ground cinnamon
¾ cup sour cream
1 cup roughly mashed banana

Preheat the oven to 180°C (350°F). Place the butter,
caster sugar and brown sugar in the bowl of an electric
mixer and beat until light and creamy. Gradually add the
eggs and beat well. Sift the flour and baking powder over
the mixture. Add the cinnamon, sour cream and banana
and stir to combine. Spoon the mixture into a greased
26cm (10 in) fluted ring tin*. Bake for 40 minutes or until
cooked when tested with a skewer. Cool on a wire rack and
spread with caramel sauce (page 96). Serves 8–10.

sour cream pound cake

250g (8 oz) butter, softened
1½ cups caster (superfine) sugar
1 teaspoon vanilla extract
6 eggs
1 cup sour cream
3 cups plain (all-purpose) flour
1½ teaspoons baking powder

Preheat the oven to 160°C (325°F). Place the butter,
sugar and vanilla in the bowl of an electric mixer and beat
until light and creamy. Gradually add the eggs and sour
cream and beat well. Sift the flour and baking powder over
the mixture and stir to combine. Spoon into a 23cm (9 in)
square cake tin lined with non-stick baking paper and bake
for 1 hour or until cooked when tested with a skewer.
Serves 8–10.

classic baked cheesecake

110g (3½ oz) plain sweet biscuits, crushed
⅔ cup almond meal
60g (2 oz) butter, melted
filling
1½ tablespoons cornflour (cornstarch)
1½ tablespoons water
330g (11 oz) cream cheese, softened
460g (15 oz) fresh ricotta cheese
4 eggs
1⅓ cups sugar
1 tablespoon finely grated lemon rind
¼ cup (2 fl oz) lemon juice

To make the base, process the biscuits in a food processor
until crushed. Add the almond meal and butter and
process until combined. Grease a 20cm (8 in) springform
tin* and line the base with non-stick baking paper. Press
the biscuit mixture over the base and refrigerate.
Preheat the oven to 150°C (300°F). To make the filling,
mix the cornflour with the water to make a smooth paste.
Process the cream cheese in a food processor until
smooth. Add the cornflour mixture, ricotta, eggs, sugar,
lemon rind and lemon juice and process until smooth.
Pour the cream cheese mixture over the base and bake for
1 hour 10 minutes or until set. Refrigerate until cold.
Serve cut into wedges with thick (double) cream. Serves 8.

classic baked cheesecake

how to chocolate truffle cake

½ cup plain (all-purpose) flour
2 tablespoons cocoa powder
⅓ cup caster (superfine) sugar
4 eggs
80g (2½ oz) butter, melted
truffle filling
450g (15 oz) dark couverture chocolate*
2 cups (16 fl oz) (single or pouring) cream
6 egg yolks
⅓ cup caster (superfine) sugar

Preheat the oven to 180°C (350°F). Sift the flour and cocoa three times and set aside. Place the sugar and eggs in the bowl of an electric mixer and beat for 8–10 minutes or until pale and thick and tripled in volume. Gently fold through the flour and cocoa and then the butter. Line the base of a 20cm (8 in) springform tin* with non-stick baking paper. Pour in the mixture and bake for 25 minutes or until the cake comes away from the side of the tin. Cool in the tin.

While the cake is cooking, make the truffle filling. Place the chocolate and cream in a saucepan over low heat and stir until melted and smooth. Place the egg yolks and sugar in a heatproof bowl over a saucepan of simmering water and beat for 6 minutes or until thick and creamy. Fold the chocolate mixture through the egg mixture and beat for 6 minutes or until cold. Refrigerate for 30 minutes.

To assemble, remove the cake from the tin and cut in half horizontally. Place the bottom layer back in the tin and pour over half of the truffle filling. Place the top layer on the cake and cover with the remaining filling. Refrigerate for 5 hours or until set. To serve, place a warm tea towel around the tin, which will help to ease the cake away from the side. Carefully remove the cake from the tin and use a heated palette knife to smooth the edge. Serves 10–12.

During cooking the cake will shrink away from the side of the tin so that when you pour the truffle filling over the top, it will spread down the side of the cake and create a great smooth and glossy coating. To smooth the edge after removing the cake from the tin, dip a palette knife into hot water, dry it quickly with a tea towel and run the blade around the edge.

chocolate truffle cake

moist chocolate cake

apricot upside-down cake

date loaf

moist chocolate cake

300g (10 oz) dark couverture chocolate*, chopped
250g (8 oz) butter
5 eggs
1/2 cup caster (superfine) sugar
1 1/4 cups plain (all-purpose) flour
1 1/4 teaspoons baking powder
3/4 cup almond meal

Preheat the oven to 150°C (300°F). Place the chocolate and butter in a saucepan over low heat and stir until melted and smooth. Set aside.
Place the eggs and sugar in the bowl of an electric mixer and beat for 8–10 minutes or until pale and thick. Sift the flour and baking powder over the egg mixture and gently fold through with the almond meal and chocolate mixture. Line the base of a 23cm (9 in) round cake tin with non-stick baking paper. Pour in the mixture and bake for 50 minutes or until cooked when tested with a skewer. Cool in the tin. Spread the cooled cake with chocolate fudge icing (page 96) if desired. Serves 10.

apricot upside-down cake

1 1/2 cups plain (all-purpose) flour
2 teaspoons baking powder
4 eggs
1 cup caster (superfine) sugar
1 teaspoon vanilla extract
125g (4 oz) butter, melted
topping
1 cup sugar
1/2 cup (4 fl oz) water
75g (2 1/2 oz) butter
12 apricots, halved and stones removed

Preheat the oven to 160°C (325°F). To make the topping, place the sugar and water in a saucepan over low heat and stir until the sugar is dissolved. Increase the heat and boil until the syrup is a golden brown colour. Remove from the heat and stir through the butter. Pour into a well greased 24cm (9 1/2 in) round cake tin.
To make the cake, sift together the flour and baking powder three times and set aside.
Place the eggs, sugar and vanilla in the bowl of an electric mixer and beat for 8–10 minutes or until thick and pale. Sift the flour and baking powder over the egg mixture and gently fold through. Fold through the butter. Place the apricots cut-side down and very close together in the caramel. Spoon over the cake mixture and bake for 1 hour 5 minutes or until cooked when tested with a skewer. Allow to stand for 5 minutes then invert the cake onto a plate. Serve warm with thick (double) cream. Serves 10.

date loaf

1 1/2 cups plain (all-purpose) flour
1 1/2 teaspoons baking powder
2/3 cup caster (superfine) sugar
1 cup roughly chopped pitted dates
1/2 cup roughly chopped pecan nuts
125g (4 oz) butter
1/4 cup (2 fl oz) milk
2 eggs

Preheat the oven to 160°C (325°F). Sift the flour and baking powder into a bowl. Add the sugar, dates and pecans and mix to combine. Set aside.
Place the butter and milk in a small saucepan over low heat and cook until just melted. Add to the flour mixture with the eggs and stir until combined. Spoon the mixture into a greased 10cm x 20cm (4 in x 8 in) loaf tin and bake for 1 hour 15 minutes or until cooked when tested with a skewer. Cool in the tin for 5 minutes then slice and serve plain or spread with butter. Serves 6–8.

blueberry swirl cheesecake

220g (7 1/2 oz) fresh or frozen blueberries
1/4 cup caster (superfine) sugar
base
85g (2 1/2 oz) shortbread biscuits
1/2 cup almond meal
45g (1 1/2 oz) butter, melted
filling
600g (20 oz) cream cheese, softened
3/4 cup sour cream
2 eggs
1 cup caster (superfine) sugar
1 teaspoon vanilla extract

Process the blueberries in a food processor and press through a sieve (you should have 1/2 cup (4 fl oz) puree). Place the puree and sugar in a small saucepan over medium heat and stir until the sugar is dissolved. Rapidly simmer for 8 minutes or until thick. Set aside to cool.
To make the base, process the biscuits in a food processor until crushed. Add the almond meal and butter and process until combined. Grease a 22cm (9 in) springform tin* and line the base with non-stick baking paper. Press the crumb mixture over the base and refrigerate.
Preheat the oven to 140°C (280°F). To make the filling, process the cream cheese in a food processor until smooth. Add the sour cream, eggs, sugar and vanilla and process until combined and smooth. Pour the cream cheese mixture over the base. Drizzle the blueberry mixture over and swirl lightly with a butter knife. Bake for 1 hour or until set. Refrigerate and serve cold. Serves 10–12.

blueberry swirl cheesecake

angel food cake

how to angel food cake

12 egg whites
1 teaspoon cream of tartar
1¼ cups caster (superfine) sugar
1 teaspoon vanilla extract
1 cup plain (all-purpose) flour

Preheat the oven to 190°C (375°F). Place the egg whites and cream of tartar in a bowl and beat with an electric mixer until soft peaks form. Add ¾ cup of the sugar, 2 tablespoons at a time, and beat well after each addition. Continue beating until thick and glossy.

Add the vanilla and beat. Sift together the flour and remaining sugar twice, then sift a third time over the egg white mixture and gently fold through. Spoon the mixture into an ungreased angel food cake tin*.

Bake for 30 minutes or until cooked when tested with a skewer. Invert the tin and allow the cake to cool completely then loosen the edge of the cake and twist the middle funnel to remove from the tin. Serve with cooled chocolate glaze (page 96) and raspberries. Serves 10–12.

Be sure to beat the egg whites and sugar very well between each addition or the cake will have a slightly gritty texture due to the undissolved sugar.
coconut angel food cake Add ½ cup desiccated coconut to the mixture when folding through the flour and remaining sugar in step 2 above.
lemon angel food cake Omit the vanilla extract and fold through 1 tablespoon finely grated lemon rind with the flour and remaining sugar in step 2 above.

fruit crumble cake   ginger cake

coconut cake with lemon syrup

fruit crumble cake

185g (6 oz) butter, softened
1¼ cups caster (superfine) sugar
1½ teaspoons vanilla extract
3 eggs
2¼ cups plain (all-purpose) flour, sifted
2 teaspoons baking powder
¼ cup (2 fl oz) milk
5 plums, stoned and thinly sliced ■
5 apricots, stoned and thinly sliced ■
caster (superfine) sugar, extra, for sprinkling
crumble topping
⅓ cup plain (all-purpose) flour
1½ tablespoons sugar
35g (1 oz) cold butter, chopped

Preheat the oven to 180°C (350°F). Place the butter,
sugar and vanilla in the bowl of an electric mixer and beat
until light and creamy. Gradually add the eggs and beat
well. Sift the flour and baking powder over the butter
mixture, add the milk and beat until combined. Grease a
20cm x 30cm (8 in x 12 in) shallow cake tin and line with
non-stick baking paper. Spoon in the mixture, arrange the
fruit over the top and sprinkle with the extra sugar.
To make the crumble topping, place the flour, sugar and
butter in a bowl and mix to combine. Scatter over the fruit.
Bake for 50 minutes or until cooked when tested with a
skewer. Serves 10.
■ Use any combination of stone fruits available.

ginger cake

1¾ cups plain (all-purpose) flour, sifted
1¾ teaspoons baking powder, sifted
¾ cup caster (superfine) sugar
125g (4 oz) butter, melted
3 eggs
¾ cup sour cream
⅓ cup golden syrup
½ cup finely chopped glacé ginger

Preheat the oven to 180°C (350°F). Place the flour, baking
powder and sugar in a bowl. Place the butter, eggs, sour
cream, golden syrup and ginger in another bowl and mix
to combine. Add the butter mixture to the dry ingredients
and stir until just combined. Spoon the mixture into a
20cm (8 in) square cake tin lined with non-stick baking
paper and bake for 50 minutes or until cooked when
tested with a skewer. Cool in the tin for 5 minutes then
turn out onto a wire rack. Serve warm or spread the
completely cooled cake with basic lemon icing (page 62)
Serves 8–10.

coconut cake with lemon syrup

125g (4 oz) butter, softened
2 teaspoons finely grated lemon rind
1 cup caster (superfine) sugar
4 eggs
2 cups desiccated coconut
1 cup plain (all-purpose) flour, sifted
1 teaspoon baking powder, sifted
lemon syrup
1 cup sugar
¼ cup (2 fl oz) lemon juice
¾ cup (6 fl oz) water
½ cup shredded lemon rind

Preheat the oven to 160°C (325°F). Place the butter,
lemon rind and sugar in the bowl of an electric mixer and
beat until light and creamy. Add the eggs gradually and
beat well. Fold through the coconut, flour and baking
powder. Pour the mixture into a 20cm (8 in) round cake
tin lined with non-stick baking paper and bake for
45 minutes or until cooked when tested with a skewer.
To make the lemon syrup, place the sugar, lemon juice,
water and lemon rind in a saucepan over low heat and
stir until the sugar is dissolved. Allow to boil for
5–7 minutes or until syrupy.
Pour half of the hot syrup over the hot cake in the tin.
Remove the cake from the tin, slice and serve with the
remaining syrup and thick (double) cream. Serves 8–10.

carrot cake

1¼ cups brown sugar
¾ cup vegetable oil
3 eggs
1½ cups plain (all-purpose) flour
1½ teaspoons baking powder
1 teaspoon bicarbonate of soda (baking soda)
1 teaspoon ground cinnamon
½ teaspoon ground ginger
2½ cups grated carrot
½ cup chopped pecan nuts
½ cup sultanas

Preheat the oven to 180°C (350°F). Place the sugar
and oil in the bowl of an electric mixer and beat for
2–3 minutes. Add the eggs gradually and beat well.
Sift the flour, baking powder, bicarbonate of soda,
cinnamon and ginger over the sugar mixture. Add the
carrot, pecans and sultanas and mix until just combined.
Pour the mixture into a greased 22cm (9 in) round
cake tin lined with non-stick baking paper and bake for
55–60 minutes or until cooked when tested with a skewer.
Serve the cake warm or cool completely and spread with
cream cheese frosting (page 96). Serves 8.

carrot cake

short order

candied citrus peel and syrup

chocolate glaze

melt-and-mix chocolate coconut cake

short order

candied citrus peel and syrup

Place 1½ cups (12 fl oz) water and 1 cup sugar in a saucepan over low heat. Stir until the sugar is dissolved. Add ½ cup shredded orange, lemon or lime rind, increase the heat and boil for 6–8 minutes or until the rind is glossy and transparent. Use the rind on its own for decoration or pour over with the warm syrup for deliciously moist cakes.

chocolate glaze

Place 150g (5 oz) chopped dark couverture chocolate* and ½ cup (4 fl oz) (single or pouring) cream in a small saucepan over low heat, stirring until melted and smooth. Allow the mixture to stand for 10 minutes and to thicken slightly. Pour the glaze over a well chilled cake and tap to remove any air bubbles or refrigerate the glaze and serve as a rich chocolate sauce with desserts.

melt-and-mix chocolate coconut cake

Preheat the oven to 180°C (350°F). Place 250g (8 oz) melted butter, ¾ cup sifted cocoa powder, 1⅓ cups caster (superfine) sugar, 3 eggs, 1½ cups desiccated coconut, 1½ cups plain (all-purpose) flour, 1½ teaspoons baking powder and ¾ cup (6 fl oz) milk in a bowl and whisk until smooth. Pour into a greased 24cm (9½ in) round cake tin lined with non-stick baking paper and bake for 50 minutes. Dust with cocoa and serve warm or cold with thick (double) cream. Serves 8–10.

cream cheese frosting

Process 250g (8 oz) softened cream cheese in a food processor until smooth. Add ⅓ cup sifted icing (confectioner's) sugar and 1½ tablespoons lemon juice and process until smooth. Use as a creamy frosting for carrot, ginger, sour cream pound, madeira or butter cakes.

butter cream frosting

Place 250g (8 oz) softened butter in the bowl of an electric mixer and beat until light and creamy. Add 1 cup sifted icing (confectioner's) sugar and 1 teaspoon vanilla extract and beat until well combined. Spread over a completely cooled cake and refrigerate until set.

melt-and-mix butter cake

Preheat the oven to 180°C (350°F). Place 1¾ cups plain (all-purpose) flour, 1¾ teaspoons baking powder, 1 cup caster (superfine) sugar, 125g (4 oz) melted butter, 2 eggs and ¼ cup (2 fl oz) milk in a bowl and mix until combined. Spoon into a 20cm (8 in) round cake tin lined with non-stick baking paper and bake for 40 minutes or until cooked when tested with a skewer. Cool in the tin for 5 minutes then invert onto a wire rack. Serves 8–10.

chocolate fudge icing

Place 250g (8 oz) dark couverture chocolate*, ½ cup (4 fl oz) (single or pouring) cream and 70g (2 oz) butter in a heatproof bowl over a saucepan of simmering water. Stir until melted and smooth. Remove and set aside to cool completely then beat with electric beaters until thick and fluffy. Spread over a chilled cake.

caramel sauce

Place ¾ cup brown sugar and 1 cup (8 fl oz) (single or pouring) cream in a saucepan over medium heat and stir until the sugar is dissolved. Increase the heat and simmer rapidly for 8 minutes or until the sauce thickens. Allow to cool until thick enough to spoon or pour over a chilled cake. Serve with banana, chocolate, carrot, ginger, coffee or caramel cakes.

cream cheese frosting

butter cream frosting

melt-and-mix butter cake

chocolate fudge icing

caramel sauce

enticing

desserts

*heavenly
sublime*

The desserts I love to make again and again – and the desserts my family and friends always ask for – don't take all day to prepare, don't involve hunting around for hard-to-find ingredients and don't mean dirtying every pan, bowl and implement in the kitchen. All I do is take a lovely ripe pear and poach it. Perfect. Or combine some chocolate, butter, cream, eggs and icing sugar for chocolate mousse in no time at all. Delicious. A luscious crème caramel might take a few moments more and a little more effort, but the results are definitely worth it.

And then there are the other classic desserts of my childhood, the summer pudding, the pavlova, the trifle and bombe Alaska, to name a few. With just slight adaptations to suit new tastes and cooking styles, they sit so well on the modern table and fulfil the ultimate dessert imperative – that wonderful silence as eager spoons scooping away at bowls do the talking.

raspberry, peach and mango sorbets

how to fruit sorbet

³/4 cup caster (superfine) sugar
1 cup (8 fl oz) water
fruit puree of your choice (see below)

To make the basic syrup, place the sugar and water in a saucepan over low heat and stir without boiling until the sugar is dissolved.

Increase the heat and bring to the boil for 1 minute. Set aside to cool. While the syrup is cooling, prepare one of the fruit variations below.

Combine the fruit puree and sugar syrup, place in an ice-cream maker and follow the manufacturer's instructions or follow the freezing instructions below for a thick and scoopable sorbet. Serves 4–6.

If you don't have an ice-cream maker, place the fruit and syrup mixture in a metal bowl or cake tin, cover and freeze for 1 hour or until just beginning to set at the edge. Beat with an electric hand mixer or a whisk and return to the freezer. Repeat three times at hourly intervals or until the sorbet is thick and smooth.

raspberry sorbet Add 1³/4 cups strained raspberry puree (700g/23 oz fresh or frozen raspberries) and ¹/4 cup (2 fl oz) lime juice to the cooled basic sorbet syrup (see above) and continue with step 3.

peach sorbet Combine 2¹/2 cups strained peach puree (6 peaches or 900g/1³/4 lb chopped peach flesh) and ¹/3 cup (2¹/2 fl oz) lemon juice to the cooled basic sorbet syrup (see above) and continue with step 3.

mango sorbet Combine 2¹/2 cups mango puree (4 x 400g/14 oz mangoes or 950g/2 lb chopped mango flesh) and ¹/2 cup (4 fl oz) lime juice to the cooled basic sorbet syrup (see above) and continue with step 3.

strawberry sorbet Add 2¹/2 cups strained strawberry puree (850g/1³/4 lb fresh strawberries) and ¹/2 cup (4 fl oz) lime juice to the cooled basic sorbet syrup (see above) and continue with step 3.

summer pudding

chocolate mousse

classic poached pear

summer pudding

1 cup caster (superfine) sugar
1/3 cup (2 1/2 fl oz) water
3 1/2 cups raspberries
1 cup redcurrants
2/3 cup blackcurrants
8 slices brioche*, lightly toasted

Place the sugar and water in a small saucepan over low heat and stir until the sugar is dissolved. Add the raspberries, redcurrants and blackcurrants and simmer for 1 minute. Pour the mixture into a sieve over a bowl and allow all of the juice to drain from the berries. Set aside to allow both the berries and liquid to cool.
To serve, place a slice of brioche on each plate, spoon over some of the berry mixture and some juice, top with the remaining brioche slices and spoon over the remaining berries and juice. Serve immediately with thick (double) cream. Serves 4.

chocolate mousse

200g (7 oz) dark couverture chocolate*, chopped
75g (2 1/2 oz) butter, chopped
4 eggs, separated
1 cup (8 fl oz) (single or pouring) cream
2 tablespoons icing (confectioner's) sugar

Place the chocolate and butter in a saucepan over low heat and stir until melted and smooth. Pour the mixture into a bowl and add the egg yolks, one at a time, beating until well combined. Set aside.
Place the cream in a bowl and whip until soft peaks form. Set aside.
Place the egg whites in a bowl and whisk until soft peaks form. Sift over the icing sugar and whisk until the mixture is thick and glossy.
Gently fold the cream through the chocolate mixture, then fold the egg whites through. Spoon into bowls and refrigerate for at least 3 hours. Serve with fresh berries if desired. Serves 6–8.

classic poached pears

2 cups (16 fl oz) red wine
2 cups (16 fl oz) water
3/4 cup sugar
1 cinnamon stick
1 clove
2 x 5cm (2 in) pieces orange rind
6 beurre bosc pears, peeled, stalks intact

Place the wine, water, sugar, cinnamon, clove and orange rind in a saucepan over medium–low heat, stirring until the sugar is dissolved. Simmer for 5 minutes then add the pears. Simmer, covered, for 30 minutes, turning the pears occasionally. Remove from the heat, remove the lid and allow the pears to cool in the pan. For an intense red colour, refrigerate the pears for a few hours or overnight in the red wine syrup. To serve, place the pears on plates with a little of the syrup. Serves 6.

peach and vanilla panna cotta

1 1/2 cups (12 fl oz) water
1/2 cup sugar
3 peaches, halved and stoned
1 tablespoon powdered gelatine
panna cotta
2 tablespoons powdered gelatine
1/3 cup (2 1/2 fl oz) water
3 3/4 cups (30 fl oz) (single or pouring) cream
1 cup icing (confectioner's) sugar
1 teaspoon vanilla extract

Place the water and sugar in a saucepan over medium heat and stir until the sugar is dissolved. Add the peaches and allow to simmer for 3–5 minutes or until soft. Remove the peaches (reserving the poaching liquid), slip off the skins and set the fruit aside.
Place 1/4 cup of the peach liquid in a bowl, sprinkle over the gelatine and set aside for 5 minutes. Add the gelatine mixture to the remaining liquid in the saucepan, stir through and simmer for 2 minutes or until dissolved. Place the peach halves, cut-side up, in a well greased 26cm x 8cm x 7.5cm (10 in x 3 1/4 x 3 in) loaf tin and pour over the liquid. Refrigerate for 2 hours or until firm. To make the panna cotta, sprinkle the gelatine over the water and set aside for 5 minutes. Place the cream, icing sugar and vanilla in a saucepan over medium heat and stir. Add the gelatine mixture and simmer over low heat for 4 minutes or until dissolved. Allow to cool to room temperature then pour the mixture over the set jelly and refrigerate for 6 hours or overnight. To serve, dip the tin into a baking dish of warm water and invert onto a plate. Slice and serve immediately. Serves 6–8.

peach and vanilla panna cotta

crème brûlée

4 cups (1³/4 pints) (single or pouring) cream
1 vanilla bean*, split and scraped
8 egg yolks
1/2 cup caster (superfine) sugar
1/4 cup caster (superfine) sugar, extra, for topping

Preheat the oven to 150°C (300°F). Place the cream and vanilla bean in a saucepan over low heat and simmer for 3 minutes. Set aside for 20 minutes.
Whisk the egg yolks and sugar until well combined.
Slowly pour over the cream mixture while whisking well to combine. Return the mixture to the saucepan and stir over medium–low heat for 6–8 minutes or until thick enough to coat the back of a spoon. Remove the vanilla bean and strain the mixture into 6 x ³/4 cup (6 fl oz) capacity ramekins*. Place the ramekins in a baking dish and pour in enough hot water to come halfway up the side of the ramekins. Bake for 15–20 minutes or until the custard is set. Remove the ramekins from the dish and refrigerate for 1 hour or until cold.
Place the ramekins on a baking tray, sprinkle with the extra sugar and allow to stand for 2 minutes. Place ice cubes in the tray around the ramekins, place under a preheated hot grill (broiler) and cook for 2–3 minutes or until the sugar is melted and golden. Alternatively, heat a large metal spoon over a cooktop or gas flame until very hot. Wearing an oven glove or using a tea towel, remove the spoon from the heat and run the back of it over the sugar on top of the custard to melt and caramelise it. Serves 6.

pink grapefruit granita

1¹/3 cups (10¹/2 fl oz) water
2/3 cup sugar
2 cups (16 fl oz) fresh pink or ruby
  grapefruit juice, strained

Place the water and sugar in a small saucepan over low heat and stir until the sugar is dissolved. Set aside to cool. Place the grapefruit juice and sugar syrup in a jug and stir to combine. Pour into a metal tray, place in the freezer and leave for 4 hours or until set.
To serve, rake the granita with a fork and spoon into chilled bowls. Serves 8.

pavlova

4 egg whites
1 cup caster (superfine) sugar
3 teaspoons cornflour (cornstarch)
1 teaspoon white vinegar

Preheat the oven to 150°C (300°F). Place the egg whites in the bowl of an electric mixer and beat until soft peaks form. Gradually add the sugar, beating well until the mixture is glossy. Sift the cornflour over the egg white mixture and fold through with the vinegar.
Pile the meringue mixture into an 18cm (7 in) round on a baking tray lined with non-stick baking paper. Place in the oven, reduce the temperature to 120°C (250°F) and cook for 1 hour. Turn the oven off and allow the meringue to cool in the oven. To serve, top with whipped cream and fresh fruit and serve immediately. Serves 6–8.

tiramisu

1/2 cup (4 fl oz) strong espresso coffee
1/2 cup (4 fl oz) coffee liqueur
16 sponge finger biscuits*, halved widthwise
cocoa powder for dusting
filling
1¹/4 cups (310g/10¹/2 oz) mascarpone*
1¹/2 cups (12 fl oz) (single or pouring) cream
3 tablespoons icing (confectioner's) sugar, sifted

To make the filling, place the mascarpone, cream and icing sugar in a bowl and whisk until light and creamy. Set aside.
Place the coffee and liqueur in a small bowl and stir to combine. Quickly dip both sides of half the biscuit halves in the coffee mixture and place in 4 glasses or small bowls. Top with half the filling. Dip the remaining biscuit halves, place on top of the cream layer and spoon over the remaining filling. Dust heavily with cocoa and refrigerate until required. Serves 4.

crème brûlée

pavlova

pink grapefruit granita

tiramisu

crème caramel

how to crème caramel

²/₃ cup caster (superfine) sugar
¹/₃ cup (2¹/₂ fl oz) water
custard
²/₃ cup (5 fl oz) milk
³/₄ cup (6 fl oz) (single or pouring) cream
2 eggs
4 egg yolks, extra
¹/₃ cup caster (superfine) sugar
1¹/₂ teaspoons vanilla extract

Preheat the oven to 150°C (300°F). Place the sugar and water in a saucepan over low heat and stir until the sugar is dissolved. Brush the sides of the pan with a little water to remove any sugar crystals. Increase the heat and boil for 8–10 minutes or until the syrup is a deep golden colour. Pour into 4 x ³/₄ cup (6 fl oz) capacity ramekins*. Set aside for 5 minutes to allow the caramel to set.

To make the custard, place the milk and cream in a saucepan over low heat and heat until warm. Place the eggs, extra egg yolks, sugar and vanilla in a bowl and whisk until well combined. Slowly pour over the milk mixture while whisking well to combine. Strain and pour over the caramel in the ramekins.

Place the ramekins in a baking tray and pour in enough hot water to come three-quarters of the way up the sides of the ramekins. Bake for 35 minutes or until the custard is set. Remove from the tray and refrigerate until cold. To serve, dip the base of each ramekin into hot water for 10 seconds, invert the crème caramel onto a plate and serve immediately. Serves 4.

orange crème caramel **Omit the vanilla extract and add 1 tablespoon orange liqueur such as Grand Marnier to the custard mixture in step 2 above.**
espresso crème caramel **Omit the vanilla extract and add 2 tablespoons strong espresso coffee liquid or 1 tablespoon instant coffee granules or powder dissolved in 1 tablespoon boiling water to the custard mixture in step 2 above.**

summer trifle

panna cotta

orange and Campari jelly

summer trifle

1 cup (8 fl oz) dessert wine
1/3 cup sugar
1 or 2 peaches, stoned and thinly sliced
1 or 2 nectarines, plums or apricots, stoned and thinly sliced
18cm (7 in) square ready-prepared sponge cake (or see page 75)
raspberry cream
1 cup (8 fl oz) (single or pouring) cream
150g (5 oz) raspberries
1 tablespoon icing (confectioner's) sugar, sifted

Place the wine and sugar in a saucepan over low heat and stir until the sugar is dissolved. Increase the heat and simmer for 5 minutes or until syrupy. Set aside to cool. Place the fruit in a bowl and pour over just enough syrup to coat the fruit slices.
Cut the cake into thick pieces and place half on plates. Spoon over half of the remaining syrup to soak the cake. To make the raspberry cream, place the cream in a chilled bowl and beat until soft peaks form. Lightly crush the raspberries with a fork and fold through the cream with the icing sugar. Spoon half of the raspberry cream over the sponge pieces and top with half of the fruit. Repeat the layers with the remaining sponge cake, syrup, raspberry cream and fruit and serve immediately. Serves 4.

panna cotta

1/4 cup (2 oz) water
3 1/2 teaspoons powdered gelatine
3 1/4 cups (26 fl oz) (single or pouring) cream
3/4 cup icing (confectioner's) sugar, sifted
1 vanilla bean*, split and scraped

Place the water in a bowl and sprinkle over the gelatine. Set aside for 5 minutes.
Place the cream, icing sugar and vanilla bean in a saucepan over medium–low heat and simmer, stirring occasionally, for 5 minutes. Add the gelatine mixture and cook, stirring, for 2 minutes. Remove the vanilla bean. Pour the mixture into 8 x 1/2 cup (4 fl oz) capacity moulds▪ and refrigerate for 4–6 hours or until set.
To serve, invert the panna cotta onto plates. Serve with berries if desired. Serves 8.
▪ You could also use small ramekins* or tea cups and serve the panna cotta in them rather than unmoulding it.

orange and Campari jelly

1/3 cup (2 1/2 fl oz) water
6 teaspoons powdered gelatine
2 3/4 cups (22 fl oz) freshly squeezed orange juice, strained
5 tablespoons caster (superfine) sugar
2/3 cup (5 fl oz) Campari
oranges in Campari syrup
1 cup caster (superfine) sugar
1/2 cup (4 fl oz) Campari
2 tablespoons water
4 oranges, peeled and sliced

Place the water in a bowl and sprinkle over the gelatine. Allow to stand for 5 minutes. Place the orange juice and sugar in a saucepan over medium heat and stir until the sugar is dissolved. Add the gelatine mixture and simmer, stirring, for 4 minutes or until clear. Remove from the heat and stir in the Campari. Pour the mixture into 8 lightly oiled 1/2 cup (4 fl oz) capacity jelly (jello) moulds or cups. Refrigerate for 2–3 hours or until set.
To make the oranges in Campari syrup, place the sugar, Campari and water in a frying pan over medium heat and stir until the sugar is dissolved. Bring to the boil and cook for 5 minutes or until thick. Remove from the heat and add the orange slices. Set aside to cool.
To serve, place the oranges on plates, spoon over some syrup and unmould the jellies on top. Serves 8.

cassata

18cm (7 in) square ready-prepared sponge cake (or see page 75)
1/2 cup (4 fl oz) orange liqueur such as Cointreau
1 cup (8 fl oz) (single or pouring) cream
grated dark chocolate to serve
filling
400g (14 oz) fresh ricotta cheese
2 tablespoons chopped glacé clementine or orange
1/4 cup chopped glacé melon
1/4 cup chopped glacé fig
2 tablespoons icing (confectioner's) sugar, sifted
1/4 cup (2 fl oz) (single or pouring) cream

To make the filling, place the ricotta, clementine, melon, fig, icing sugar and cream in a bowl and mix to combine. Cut the cake into 1.5cm (2/3 in) thick slices then cut these into 5cm (2 in) squares. Place a cake square on each plate, brush well with the liqueur and spread with a thick layer of the ricotta mixture. Place another piece of cake on top and repeat the layers, finishing with a piece of sponge cake. To serve, whip the cream until it forms soft peaks. Spread over the cake layers and sprinkle with the chocolate. Serves 8.

cassata

how to vanilla ice cream

1 cup (8 fl oz) milk
2 cups (16 fl oz) (single or pouring) cream
1 vanilla bean*, split and scraped
6 egg yolks
2/3 cup caster (superfine) sugar

Place the milk, cream and vanilla bean in a saucepan over medium heat and heat, stirring occasionally, until hot but not boiling. Remove from the heat and set aside.

Place the egg yolks and sugar in a bowl and whisk until thick and pale. Remove the vanilla bean from the milk mixture and slowly pour over the egg yolk and sugar mixture while whisking well to combine.

Pour the mixture back into the saucepan and stir over a low heat for 4 minutes or until the custard is thick and coats the back of a spoon. Set aside to cool then place in an ice-cream maker and follow the manufacturer's instructions for thick and scoopable ice cream or follow the freezing instructions below. Makes 1 litre (32 fl oz).

If you don't have an ice-cream maker, place the mixture in a metal bowl or cake tin, cover and freeze for 1 hour or until just beginning to set at the edge. Beat with an electric hand mixer or a whisk and return to the freezer. Repeat three times at hourly intervals or until the ice cream is thick, smooth and scoopable.

pistachio ice cream Replace the vanilla bean with 1 teaspoon vanilla extract and add 1 cup roasted and chopped pistachio nuts to the churned basic vanilla ice cream.

chocolate chip ice cream Replace the vanilla bean with 1 teaspoon vanilla extract and add 1 cup chopped dark chocolate to the churned basic vanilla ice cream.

maple syrup ice cream Replace the vanilla bean with 1 teaspoon vanilla extract. Simmer 3/4 cup maple syrup until reduced to 1/2 cup and add to the milk mixture in step 1 then continue with the basic recipe.

praline ice cream Replace the vanilla bean with 1 teaspoon vanilla extract and make one quantity of praline (page 124) and stir through the churned basic ice cream.

basic vanilla ice cream (middle left) and (clockwise)
chocolate chip, maple syrup, pistachio and praline variations

amaretti and orange curd parfait

triple chocolate semifreddo

bombe Alaska

amaretti and orange curd parfait

2 cups (16 fl oz) (single or pouring) cream
1/3 cup icing (confectioner's) sugar, sifted
2 tablespoons Grand Marnier liqueur
200g (7 oz) ready-prepared amaretti biscuits* (or see page 36)
1 quantity orange curd (page 124)

Place the cream, icing sugar and liqueur in a bowl and whisk until soft peaks form. Chop the biscuits into pieces. Spoon half of the orange curd then half of the cream into four glasses. Top with the biscuit pieces, spoon over the remaining cream and drizzle over the remaining orange curd. Refrigerate for 2 hours before serving. Serves 4.

triple chocolate semifreddo

250g (8 oz) dark couverture chocolate*, chopped
3 eggs
2 egg yolks, extra
1/2 cup caster (superfine) sugar
13/4 cups (14 fl oz) (single or pouring) cream
1/2 cup chopped white chocolate
1/2 cup chopped milk chocolate

Place the dark couverture chocolate in a heatproof bowl over a saucepan of simmering water and stir until melted and smooth. Set aside.
Place the eggs, extra yolks and sugar in a heatproof bowl over a saucepan of simmering water and whisk for 4–5 minutes or until the mixture is thick and pale. Remove from the heat and beat with an electric mixer for 5–6 minutes or until cool. Fold through the melted dark chocolate and set aside.
Place the cream in the bowl of an electric mixer and beat until soft peaks form. Fold the egg and chocolate mixture and the white and milk chocolate through the cream. Pour the mixture into a metal bowl or cake tin, cover and freeze for 4–6 hours or until firm.
To serve, place scoops of the semifreddo into chilled bowls. Serves 6–8.

bombe Alaska

500ml (16 fl oz) vanilla ice cream ■
18cm (7 in) square ready-prepared sponge cake (or see page 75)
1/3 cup (21/2 fl oz) framboise* or liqueur of your choice
2 egg whites
1/2 cup caster (superfine) sugar

Press the ice cream into 4 x 1/2 cup (4 fl oz) capacity moulds then turn out onto a baking tray lined with non-stick baking paper. Freeze until the ice cream is firm. Cut pieces of the sponge cake to fit under the base of the ice cream and use a spatula to slide them under. Cut the remaining cake into thin slices and use to wrap around the ice cream to enclose it completely. Brush the cake covering the ice cream well with the liqueur. Place in the freezer and leave for at least 1 hour.
Just before serving, preheat the oven to 220°C (425°F). Place the egg whites in the bowl of an electric mixer and beat until soft peaks form. Gradually add the sugar and beat until glossy. Spread over the cake-covered ice cream and bake in the top of the oven for 4–5 minutes or until the meringue is set and is a golden colour at the edges. Serve immediately. Serves 4.
■ Use any flavour of quality ice cream (or make your own, see page 116) and choose a liqueur or any type of alcohol that goes well with it.

poached summer fruits

4 peaches
4 nectarines
4 apricots
2²/3 cups raspberries
2²/3 cups blueberries
syrup
2 cups (16 fl oz) water
1 cup sugar
1 vanilla bean*, split and scraped

To blanch the stone fruit, bring a saucepan full of water to the boil and place the peaches, nectarines and apricots in it, a few at a time, for 30–60 seconds. Carefully remove the skins and set the fruit aside.
To make the syrup, place the water, sugar and vanilla bean in a saucepan over medium heat and stir until the sugar is dissolved. Simmer until the liquid is reduced by half.
Pour the hot syrup over the blanched fruit and allow to cool. To serve, toss the raspberries and blueberries through the stone fruit and place in bowls. Remove the vanilla bean and spoon over the syrup. Serves 4.

poached summer fruits

short order

berries and figs in vanilla syrup   affogato

sugar grilled fruit

short order

berries and figs in vanilla syrup

Place 1 cup (8 fl oz) water, 1/2 cup sugar and 1 vanilla bean* in a saucepan and stir over low heat until the sugar is dissolved. Increase the heat and boil for 5 minutes. Allow to cool and pour the syrup over mixed berries and halved fresh figs. Serve with thick (double) cream or ice cream.

affogato

Place scoops of vanilla ice cream in the bottom of small glasses. Pour over a little chilled chocolate or coffee liqueur and top with a shot of freshly made espresso coffee. Serve immediately.

sugar grilled fruit

Stone and slice any summer fruit of your choice (try halved peaches and apricots or mango cheeks) and press the cut side into some sugar. Place in a non-stick frying pan over medium heat and cook for 3–5 minutes or until the sugar is melted and golden. Cool slightly and serve with brown sugar mascarpone (page 174) or vanilla ice cream.

lemon, orange or passionfruit curd

Place 1/2 cup (4 fl oz) lemon or orange juice or 1/2 cup passionfruit pulp and 100g (3 1/2 oz) butter in a saucepan over low heat and stir until the butter is melted. Whisk 1/2 cup sugar, 1 egg and 3 extra egg yolks into the butter. Stir constantly over medium–low heat for 5–7 minutes or until the mixture thickens slightly. Use to fill cakes or serve with meringues. Makes 1 1/2 cups.

crepes

Sift 2 cups plain (all-purpose) flour into a bowl and add 2 tablespoons caster (superfine) sugar. Combine 4 eggs, 1 2/3 cups (13 fl oz) milk and 3/4 cup (6 fl oz) (single or pouring) cream and slowly whisk into the flour until smooth. Allow to stand for 20 minutes. Cook the crepes in a small non-stick frying pan over medium heat until light golden on each side. Serve warm. Makes 20.

praline

Preheat the oven to 180°C (350°F). Place 1/3 cup blanched almonds on a baking tray lined with non-stick baking paper and bake for 10 minutes or until golden. Place 1/2 cup caster (superfine) sugar and 1/4 cup (2 fl oz) water in a saucepan over low heat and stir until the sugar is dissolved. Increase the heat and boil the mixture until a golden colour. Remove from the heat, allow the bubbles to subside and pour over the almonds. When set, break the praline into chunks, chop into rough pieces or process in a food processor to a fine powder. Sprinkle over ice cream, cakes or desserts.

chocolate truffles

Place 1/2 cup (4 fl oz) (single or pouring) cream in a saucepan over medium heat and bring almost to the boil. Add 300g (10 oz) chopped dark couverture chocolate* and stir for 1 minute. Remove from the heat and stir until smooth. Pour into a greased 15cm (6 in) square cake tin lined with non-stick baking paper and refrigerate for 2 hours or until firm. To serve, cut into squares and dust with cocoa powder. Makes 16.

raspberry fool

Place 1 cup raspberries in a frying pan and lightly crush with a fork. Add 2/3 cup caster (superfine) sugar and 2 teaspoons lemon juice and cook over medium–low heat, stirring gently, until the sugar is dissolved. Simmer for 3 minutes or until the raspberries are soft and the juices are syrupy. Refrigerate until cold. Beat 1 1/2 cups (12 fl oz) (single or pouring) cream until soft peaks form. Fold through the raspberry mixture with 1/2 cup whole fresh raspberries. To serve, spoon into glasses. Serves 4.

lemon curd

crepes

praline

chocolate truffles

raspberry fool

comforting
hot puddings
filling

lovely

A bowl of hot pudding is to comfort what a sofa and warm socks are to a wintry Sunday evening. Essential. And the hot pudding is completely at home among the commonsense cookery classics. Simple to make and loved by everyone, a fluffy lemon delicious, a creamy baked custard or a crunchy but soft bread and butter pudding are the spontaneous cook's best friends. Chances are the ingredients will be in your kitchen no matter when the hot pudding whim hits.

Feel like a variation on the theme? Add some blueberries to your apple crumble, use stone fruits and panettone for your Christmas pudding and make your rice sticky – all great ways to update the humble pudding's image without sacrificing its basic tasty appeal. Now, close your eyes, say the word 'pudding' and see if your mouth doesn't water and happy childhood memories don't come flooding back.

how to lemon soufflés

butter, softened, for greasing
caster (superfine) sugar for dusting
100ml (3$^1\!/_2$ fl oz) lemon juice
$^2\!/_3$ cup caster (superfine) sugar
2 tablespoons water
1 tablespoon cornflour (cornstarch)
2 teaspoons water, extra
5 egg whites
$^1\!/_3$ cup caster (superfine) sugar, extra

Lightly grease 4 x $^3\!/_4$ cup (6 fl oz) capacity ceramic ramekins* with butter and dust with sugar.
Cut non-stick baking paper into strips and tie around the ramekins to make collars that stand 3cm (1$^1\!/_4$ in) above the rim. Place the ramekins well apart on a baking tray.

Place the lemon juice, sugar and water in a small saucepan over low heat and stir until the sugar is dissolved. Increase the heat and bring to the boil.
Combine the cornflour with the extra water and mix to a smooth paste. Add to the pan and cook for 1 minute, stirring continuously. Refrigerate the mixture until cold.

Preheat the oven to 180°C (350°F). Place the egg whites in the bowl of an electric mixer and beat until soft peaks form. Add the extra sugar in a thin stream, beating until glossy. Place the lemon mixture in a large bowl and gently fold through the egg white mixture. Spoon into the ramekins and bake for 12–15 minutes or until risen and golden. Gently remove the collars and serve immediately. Makes 4.

passionfruit soufflés **Replace the lemon juice with 150ml (5 fl oz) strained passionfruit pulp (about 10 passionfruit) and reduce the quantity of caster (superfine) sugar added in step 2 above to $^1\!/_4$ cup, then continue with the recipe.**
raspberry soufflés **Replace the lemon juice with 150ml (5 fl oz) strained raspberry puree (350g/12 oz fresh or frozen raspberries) and reduce the quantity of caster (superfine) sugar added in step 2 above to $^1\!/_4$ cup, then continue with the recipe.**

lemon soufflés

stone fruits Christmas pudding

ginger puddings

plum clafouti

stone fruits Christmas pudding

1 large (750g/1½ lb) panettone* or pandoro*
¾ cup (6 fl oz) dessert wine or marsala
3 peaches, stoned and sliced
3 nectarines, stoned and sliced
3 plums, stoned and sliced
3 apricots, stoned and sliced
¼ cup demerara sugar*

Preheat the oven to 200°C (400°F). Line a 26cm x 30cm (10 in x 12 in) baking dish with non-stick baking paper. Cut the pannetone into 2cm (¾ in) thick slices and place in the base of the baking dish. Sprinkle with half of the wine and scatter the fruit on top. Sprinkle with the remaining wine and the sugar. Bake for 30–35 minutes or until the fruit is soft and a golden colour.
Serve warm or cold in large wedges with thick (double) cream or vanilla ice cream. Serves 6.
■ Use any combination of summer fruit or berries to make this pudding, which is a great way to use leftover pannetone or pandoro at Christmas.

ginger puddings

75g (2½ oz) butter, softened
⅔ cup golden syrup
2 eggs
1⅓ cups plain (all-purpose) flour
2 teaspoons baking powder
¾ teaspoon bicarbonate of soda (baking soda)
½ cup finely chopped glacé ginger

Preheat the oven to 180°C (350°F). Place the butter and golden syrup in the bowl of an electric mixer and beat for 5 minutes or until light and well combined. Add the eggs gradually and beat well. Sift the flour, baking powder and bicarbonate of soda over the egg mixture and stir to combine. Stir through the ginger. Grease 6 x 1 cup (8 fl oz) capacity ovenproof dishes. Spoon in the mixture, place the dishes in a baking tray and pour in enough hot water to come halfway up the sides of the dishes. Bake for 30 minutes or until cooked when tested with a skewer. Serve warm with brandy butter (page 150). Makes 6.

plum clafouti

butter, softened, for greasing
caster (superfine) sugar for dusting
7 blood plums (400g/14 oz), halved and stoned
⅓ cup plain (all-purpose) flour
⅓ cup caster (superfine) sugar
1 teaspoon vanilla extract
1 cup (8 fl oz) (single or pouring) cream
3 eggs

Preheat the oven to 180°C (350°F). Grease an 8 cup (3½ pint) capacity ovenproof dish with butter and dust with sugar. Place the plums in the dish, cut-side up. Place the flour, sugar and vanilla in a bowl. Add the cream and whisk to combine. Add the eggs and whisk until smooth. Pour the mixture around the plums in the dish and bake for 35–40 minutes or until the pudding is puffed and golden. Serve hot with vanilla ice cream. Serves 6.

sticky toffee date pudding

200g (7 oz) pitted dates, finely chopped
⅓ cup (2½ oz) boiling water
100g (3½ oz) butter, softened
1 cup caster (superfine) sugar
2 eggs
1½ cups plain (all-purpose) flour
1½ teaspoons baking powder
¼ cup (2 fl oz) milk
toffee sauce
200g (7 oz) butter, chopped
1 cup (8 fl oz) (single or pouring) cream
1⅔ cups brown sugar

Place the dates in a bowl and pour over the boiling water. Set aside until the water has been absorbed.
Preheat the oven to 180°C (350°F). Place the butter and sugar in the bowl of an electric mixer and beat until light and creamy. Add the eggs gradually and beat well. Sift the flour and baking powder over the mixture, add the milk and dates and stir to combine. Spoon the mixture into a greased 20cm (8 in) square cake tin and bake for 40 minutes or until cooked when tested with a skewer. While the pudding is cooking, make the toffee sauce. Place the butter, cream and sugar in a saucepan over low heat and stir until the sugar is dissolved. Increase the heat and simmer rapidly for 5–8 minutes or until the sauce is thick. To serve, cut the pudding into thick slices and pour over the warm toffee sauce. Serves 6.

sticky toffee date pudding

figs with grilled honey and marsala sabayon

4 large figs, halved lengthwise
5 egg yolks
2 tablespoons caster (superfine) sugar
2 tablespoons honey
1/3 cup (2 1/2 oz) marsala

Grease 4 ovenproof dishes and stand 2 fig halves upright in each one.
To make the honey and marsala sabayon, place the egg yolks, sugar, honey and marsala in a heatproof bowl over a saucepan of simmering water and whisk or beat with an electric hand mixer for 7–8 minutes or until the mixture is thick and forms ribbon-like trails. Remove from the heat and beat for 3–4 minutes or until the mixture has cooled slightly. Spoon the sabayon over the figs. Place under a preheated hot grill (broiler) and cook for 2–3 minutes or until the tops are golden. Serve immediately. Serves 4.

lemon delicious puddings

40g (1 1/2 oz) butter, softened
3/4 cup caster (superfine) sugar
1 teaspoon finely grated lemon rind
2 eggs, separated
2 tablespoons plain (all-purpose) flour
1/2 teaspoon baking powder
1/3 cup (2 1/2 fl oz) lemon juice
1 cup (8 fl oz) milk

Preheat the oven to 180°C (350°F). Place the butter and sugar in the bowl of an electric mixer and beat until pale. Add the lemon rind and egg yolks and beat until smooth. Sift the flour and baking powder over the mixture and beat to combine. Add the lemon juice and milk and beat until smooth.
Place the egg whites in a bowl and whisk until stiff peaks form. Fold into the lemon mixture. Grease 4 large ovenproof tea cups or 4 x 1 1/2 cup (12 fl oz) capacity ramekins*. Pour in the mixture and place in a baking tray. Pour enough hot water into the tray to come halfway up the side of the cups. Bake for 20–25 minutes or until risen and golden. Makes 4.

rum and raisin puddings

2 1/2 cups raisins
2/3 cup (5 fl oz) dark rum
125g (4 oz) butter, very well softened
1 cup brown sugar
1 teaspoon vanilla extract
2 eggs
1 1/2 cups plain (all-purpose) flour
1 1/2 teaspoons baking powder
1/4 cup (2 fl oz) milk
1/3 cup (2 1/2 fl oz) dark rum, extra

Preheat the oven to 160°C (325°F). Place the raisins and rum in a small saucepan over low heat and cook until the liquid is absorbed. Set aside.
Place the butter, sugar and vanilla in the bowl of an electric mixer and beat until pale. Add the eggs gradually and beat well. Sift over the flour and baking powder, add the milk and stir to combine. Add half of the raisins and stir through.
Grease 6 x 1 cup (8 fl oz) capacity muffin tins. Spoon in the mixture and bake for 35 minutes or until risen and golden. Pour the extra rum over the remaining raisins and serve with the warm puddings and custard. Makes 6.

nectarine and blueberry gratin

6 nectarines, stoned and thickly sliced
3/4 cup blueberries
2 tablespoons sugar
40g (1 1/2 oz) butter, finely chopped
gratin topping
2 tablespoons plain (all-purpose) flour
3/4 cup almond meal
1/3 cup caster (superfine) sugar
4 egg whites

Preheat the oven to 180°C (350°F). Divide the nectarines and blueberries between 4 x 1 1/2 cup (12 fl oz) capacity ovenproof baking dishes and sprinkle with the sugar and butter.
To make the gratin topping, place the flour, almond meal and sugar in a bowl and stir to combine. Place the egg whites in a separate bowl and whisk until soft peaks form. Fold the egg whites through the flour mixture.
Drizzle the gratin topping over the fruit and bake for 25–30 minutes or until the topping is a golden colour. Serve warm or cold with thick (double) cream or vanilla ice cream. Makes 4.

figs with grilled honey and marsala sabayon

rum and raisin pudding

lemon delicious pudding

nectarine and blueberry gratin

Christmas pudding

$how\ to$ Christmas pudding

3/4 cup sultanas

1 cup currants

1 1/2 cups raisins, halved

3/4 cup pitted prunes or dates, chopped

2/3 cup candied mixed peel

2/3 cup slivered almonds

1/2 cup brandy or sherry

250g (8 oz) butter, softened

1/4 cup brown sugar

1/4 cup sugar

3 eggs

1 cup plain (all-purpose) flour, sifted

1 teaspoon ground cinnamon

1 teaspoon mixed spice

250g (8 oz) fresh breadcrumbs

150ml (5 fl oz) milk

plain (all-purpose) flour, extra, for rubbing

Place the sultanas, currants, raisins, prunes, mixed peel, almonds and brandy in a bowl and allow to soak for at least 4 hours or overnight. Place the butter, brown sugar and sugar in the bowl of an electric mixer and beat until light and creamy. Add the eggs gradually and beat well. Transfer the mixture to a large bowl. Add the fruit mixture, flour, cinnamon, mixed spice, breadcrumbs and milk and mix with a wooden spoon until well combined.

Wearing gloves, dip an 80cm (30 in) square of calico into boiling water and carefully squeeze to remove any excess water. While the cloth is still hot, rub with the extra flour to form a large circle. Place the mixture in the middle and gather up the ends of the cloth firmly around it.

Tie the cloth with string as close to the mixture as possible, making a loop at the end of the string. Place the pudding in a large saucepan of boiling water and boil for 4 hours 30 minutes, adding more water if necessary. Remove from the pan and hang on a broomstick over a sink. Allow to cool. Store in the fridge for up to 2 months. To reheat, boil for 45 minutes. Drain for 5 minutes. Unwrap and serve with brandy and vanilla custard (page 150). Serves 12.

steamed jam pudding

apple and blueberry crumble

chocolate fudge puddings

steamed jam pudding

1/3 cup raspberry or strawberry jam (jelly)
150g (5 oz) butter, softened
2/3 cup caster (superfine) sugar
2 eggs
1 teaspoon vanilla extract
2 cups plain (all-purpose) flour
2 teaspoons baking powder
2 tablespoons golden syrup
1 cup (8 fl oz) milk

Place the jam in the base of a greased 7 cup (3 pint) capacity pudding basin. Place the butter, sugar, eggs, vanilla, flour, baking powder, golden syrup and milk in the bowl of an electric mixer and beat until well combined. Spoon the mixture into the basin and place a round of greaseproof paper over the surface of the pudding. Place two pieces of aluminium foil over the top of the basin and secure with string. Place in a saucepan and pour in enough boiling water to come halfway up the side of the basin. Cover and boil, topping up the water level when necessary, for 2 hours 45 minutes or until the pudding is springy to touch.
To serve, invert the hot pudding onto a serving plate. Cut into wedges and serve with thick (double) cream or ice cream. Serves 6–8.

apple and blueberry crumble

7 green apples (1.2kg/2 lb 7 oz), cored and chopped
1 cup fresh blueberries
1/3 cup sugar
1 teaspoon finely grated lemon rind
2 teaspoons lemon juice
topping
1 cup rolled oats
1/2 cup brown sugar
1/4 cup plain (all-purpose) flour
75g (2 1/2 oz) butter, softened
1/2 teaspoon ground cinnamon

Preheat the oven to 180°C (350°F). Place the apples, blueberries, sugar, lemon rind and lemon juice in a bowl and stir to combine. Transfer to a large ovenproof dish. To make the topping, place the rolled oats, sugar, flour, butter and cinnamon in a bowl and mix to combine. Spoon the oat mixture over the fruit and bake for 55 minutes or until the topping is dark golden and crisp and the apple is soft. Serve warm with thick (double) cream or ice cream if desired. Serves 4.

chocolate fudge puddings

185g (6 oz) quality dark chocolate, chopped
185g (6 oz) butter
4 eggs, separated
1/2 cup sugar
1/2 cup almond meal
3 tablespoons plain (all-purpose) flour
3 tablespoons sugar, extra

Preheat the oven to 180°C (350°F). Place the chocolate and butter in a saucepan over very low heat and stir until melted and smooth. Set aside.
Place the egg yolks and sugar in a bowl and beat until light and creamy. Add the chocolate mixture, almond meal and flour and fold through.
Place the egg whites in a bowl and beat until soft peaks form. Add the extra sugar gradually and continue beating until the mixture is glossy. Fold the egg whites through the chocolate mixture.
Grease 6 ovenproof tea cups or 6 x 1 cup (8 fl oz) capacity ramekins*. Pour in the mixture and place in a baking dish. Pour enough hot water into the dish to come halfway up the side of the cups. Bake in a preheated oven for 25 minutes or until cooked at the edges but a little soft in the middle. Serve with thick (double) cream. Makes 6.

baked quinces

4 quinces (1.3kg/2 1/2 lb), peeled and halved
5 cups (2 pints) water
5 cups sugar
5 pieces lemon rind
2 tablespoons lemon juice
1 vanilla bean*

Preheat the oven to 200°C (400°F). Place the quinces, water, sugar, lemon rind, lemon juice and vanilla bean in a deep baking tray. Cover with aluminium foil and bake for 1 hour. Turn the quinces, cover with the aluminium foil again and return to the oven for a further 1 hour or until soft. Serve warm with a little of the syrup and thick (double) cream if desired. Serves 4.

baked quinces

how to classic baked custard

1 cup (8 fl oz) milk
1 cup (8 fl oz) (single or pouring) cream
2 eggs
2 egg yolks, extra
1/2 cup caster (superfine) sugar
1 1/2 teaspoons vanilla extract
freshly grated nutmeg

Preheat the oven to 150°C (300°F). Place the milk and cream in a saucepan over medium heat and heat until hot but not boiling.

Place the eggs, egg yolks, sugar and vanilla in a bowl and whisk until well combined. Slowly pour over the hot milk mixture, whisking well to combine.

Grease 6 x 1/2 cup (4 fl oz) capacity ovenproof dishes ▪. Pour the mixture into the dishes through a strainer and sprinkle with nutmeg. Place in a baking tray and pour in enough hot water to come halfway up the side of the dishes. Bake for 35 minutes ▪ or until just set. Serve warm or cold. Makes 6.

baked rice custard **Place 2 tablespoons cooked short-grain rice in the ovenproof dishes before pouring in the custard mixture in step 3 above.**

baked chocolate custard **Heat 100g (3 1/2 oz) chopped dark chocolate with the milk and cream in step 1 above, then continue with the recipe, omitting the nutmeg in step 3.**

baked coconut custard **Replace the milk with 1 cup (8 fl oz) coconut milk in step 1 above, then continue with the recipe, omitting the nutmeg in step 3.**

baked brown sugar custard **Replace the caster (superfine) sugar with 1/2 cup dark brown sugar in step 2 above, then continue with the recipe. Replace the nutmeg with ground cinnamon in step 3 if desired.**

▪ **Alternatively, you could use 4 x 3/4 cup (6 fl oz) capacity ovenproof dishes and bake the custards for 40 minutes.**

classic baked custard (front left) and (clockwise)
brown sugar, rice, chocolate and coconut variations

marmalade bread and butter pudding

10 slices bread, crusts removed
butter for spreading
1/3 cup bitter orange marmalade
3 cups (24 fl oz) milk
3 eggs
1/2 cup sugar
1 teaspoon vanilla extract
sugar, extra, for sprinkling

Preheat the oven to 160°C (325°F). Spread one side of five of the bread slices with butter and the remaining five slices with marmalade. Sandwich together a buttered slice and one spread with marmalade, then cut each sandwich into 3 long strips. Place in a greased 4 cup (2 pint) capacity ovenproof dish, making a rough lattice pattern. Place the milk, eggs, sugar and vanilla in a bowl and whisk to combine. Pour over the bread and allow to stand for 3 minutes. Sprinkle over some extra sugar and place the dish in a baking tray. Pour in enough hot water to come halfway up the side of the dish and bake for 1 hour 5 minutes or until the pudding is set. Allow to stand for 5 minutes and serve warm. Serves 6.

chocolate malt self-saucing pudding

135g (4 1/2 oz) butter, softened
1 1/4 cups caster (superfine) sugar
2 eggs
1 1/2 cups plain (all-purpose) flour
2 1/4 teaspoons baking powder
1/2 cup cocoa powder
1/2 cup hazelnut meal*
1/4 cup malted milk powder
1 cup (8 fl oz) milk
malted milk powder, extra, for sprinkling
sauce
2/3 cup brown sugar
2/3 cup malted milk powder
1 1/2 tablespoons cocoa powder
1 1/2 cups (12 fl oz) boiling water

Preheat the oven to 170°C (330°F). Place the butter and sugar in the bowl of an electric mixer and beat until pale. Add the eggs gradually and beat until smooth. Sift the flour, baking powder and cocoa over the mixture, add the hazelnut meal, malted milk powder and milk and beat until smooth. Spoon the mixture into a greased 8 cup (3 1/2 pint) capacity ovenproof baking dish. To make the sauce, place the sugar, malted milk powder and cocoa in a bowl, pour over the boiling water and stir to combine. Spoon over the pudding mixture and bake for 45–50 minutes or until risen and cooked when tested with a skewer. Sprinkle with some extra malted milk powder and serve warm with thick (double) cream if desired. Serves 6.

marmalade bread and butter pudding

chocolate malt self-saucing pudding

short order

brandy and vanilla custard

crème anglaise

sticky rice

short order

brandy and vanilla custard

Heat 3 cups (24 fl oz) (single or pouring) cream, 1/4 cup (2 fl oz) brandy and 1 split and scraped vanilla bean* or 1 teaspoon vanilla extract in a saucepan over medium heat until hot but not boiling. Whisk together 6 egg yolks and 1/3 cup caster (superfine) sugar. In a separate bowl, mix 2 tablespoons cornflour (cornstarch) and 1/3 cup (21/2 fl oz) milk to a smooth paste. Slowly pour the cream mixture over the egg mixture, whisking well. Whisk in the cornflour mixture until combined. Return to the saucepan and stir over low heat for 4 minutes or until thick. Serve warm. Makes 31/2 cups.

crème anglaise

Heat 1 cup (8 fl oz) milk, 1 cup (8 fl oz) (single or pouring) cream and 1 split and scraped vanilla bean* or 1 teaspoon vanilla extract in a saucepan over medium heat until hot but not boiling. Whisk together 6 egg yolks and 2 tablespoons caster (superfine) sugar. Slowly pour over the milk mixture, whisking well to combine. Return to the saucepan and stir over low heat for 5–6 minutes or until thick enough to coat the back of a spoon. Strain, cover and refrigerate. Makes 21/4 cups.

sticky rice

Bring 1 cup long-grain rice and 13/4 cups (14 fl oz) water to the boil in a saucepan and cook until tunnels form. Cover with a tightfitting lid and set aside for 10 minutes. Separate the grains with a fork and stir through 1/2 cup (4 fl oz) coconut milk and 2 tablespoons caster (superfine) sugar. Serve sprinkled with brown sugar. Serves 4.

brandy butter

Beat 250g (8 oz) softened butter, 2/3 cup sifted icing (confectioner's) sugar, 2 tablespoons brandy and 1 teaspoon vanilla extract in the bowl of an electric mixer for 7–10 minutes or until light and creamy. Serve with ginger or Christmas puddings. Serves 8.

individual Christmas puddings

Prepare the pudding mixture and 8 x 30cm (12 in) square pudding cloths according to the recipe on page 139. Place 250g (8 oz) of mixture in the centre of each pudding cloth and tie as shown on page 139. Boil the puddings for 1 hour 30 minutes, remove from the pan and hang in a cool, dry place until dry. To serve, reheat the puddings in a saucepan of boiling water for 30 minutes. Unwrap and serve with brandy and vanilla custard (this page). Makes 8.

cinnamon baked apples

Preheat the oven to 160°C (325°F). Bake 1/3 cup flaked almonds on a baking tray for 5 minutes or until golden. Set aside to cool. Core 6 apples and make a ridge around the middle using a paring knife. Combine the almonds, 1 tablespoon sugar, 1 tablespoon plain (all-purpose) flour, 10g (1/2 oz) softened butter and a pinch of ground cinnamon and spoon into the apples. Insert a cinnamon stick in each apple and bake for 25 minutes or until the apples are just soft. Serve warm with thick (double) cream or crème anglaise (this page). Makes 6.

dried fruit compote

Place 1 cup dried apricots, 1 cup dried apple, 11/4 cups (10 fl oz) freshly squeezed orange juice, 11/2 cups (12 fl oz) water, 2 cinnamon sticks and 3 pieces lemon rind in a saucepan over medium heat. Simmer rapidly for 10 minutes. Add 1/2 cup prunes and 1/2 cup dried peaches and cook for 10 minutes or until just soft. Serves 4.

zabaglione

Place 4 egg yolks, 1/4 cup caster (superfine) sugar and 1/2 cup (4 fl oz) marsala in a heatproof bowl over a saucepan of simmering water. Whisk or beat with electric beaters until thick and forming ribbon-like trails. Carefully remove the bowl from the saucepan and beat for 1 minute. Serve immediately with berries or fruit. Serves 4.

brandy butter

individual Christmas puddings

cinnamon baked apples

dried fruit compote

zabaglione

sweet
pies + tarts
special
delicious

Watch someone bite into a luscious little homemade lemon meringue pie. From the first mouthful to the picking up of the stray pastry crumbs on the fingertips, eating one is a great experience, and it shows. And so is making a pie or tart. There's something quite special, and I can't explain exactly what, about rolling out the pastry for a custard tart, or brushing the top of an apple pie and sliding it into the oven, or the fantastic smell as you open the oven again to take out your freshly baked masterpiece.

Fruity, creamy or nutty, open or closed, large or small, traditional or with a modern edge, there's a pie or tart to suit every baking urge or entertaining need. It's just a matter of teaming some pecans, peaches, plums, pears, crème pâtissière or whatever takes your fancy with some light and sweet shortcrust pastry, and you really do have it made.

sweet shortcrust pastry

how to sweet shortcrust pastry

2 cups plain (all-purpose) flour
3 tablespoons caster (superfine) sugar
150g (5 oz) cold butter, chopped
2–3 tablespoons iced water

Process the flour, sugar and butter in a food processor until the mixture resembles fine breadcrumbs. While the motor is running, add enough iced water to form a smooth dough and process until just combined. Knead the dough lightly, wrap in plastic wrap and refrigerate for 30 minutes.

Roll out the pastry on a lightly floured surface or between sheets of non-stick baking paper until 2–3mm (1/8 in) thick, or whatever thickness required, and line the tart tin. (This recipe makes about 350g (12 oz) pastry, which is sufficient to line up to a 26cm (10 in) pie dish or tart tin.)

Preheat the oven to 180°C (350°F). Place a piece of non-stick baking paper over the pastry and fill with baking weights or uncooked rice or beans. Bake for 10 minutes, remove the weights and bake for a further 10 minutes or until the pastry is golden. Spoon in the filling and bake again as the recipe indicates.

almond sweet shortcrust pastry **Add 1/2 cup almond meal with the flour in step 1 above then continue with the recipe.**
hazelnut sweet shortcrust pastry **Add 1/2 cup hazelnut meal* with the flour in step 1 above then continue with the recipe.**

pumpkin pie

pear and rhubarb pies

lemon tart

pumpkin pie

1 quantity sweet shortcrust pastry (page 157)
1 cup pureed cooked butternut pumpkin ▪
1/3 cup brown sugar
2 eggs
1/3 cup (21/2 fl oz) (single or pouring) cream
1/4 teaspoon ground cinnamon
freshly grated nutmeg for serving

Preheat the oven to 180°C (350°F). Roll out the pastry on
a lightly floured surface until 3mm (1/8 in) thick. Place in
a 22cm (9 in) tart ring*. Line the pastry with non-stick
baking paper and fill with pastry weights or uncooked rice
or beans. Bake for 10 minutes, remove the weights and
bake for a further 10 minutes or until the pastry is golden.
Reduce the oven temperature to 150°C (300°F).
To make the filling, place the pumpkin, sugar, eggs, cream
and cinnamon in a bowl and whisk to combine. Pour into
the tart shell and bake for 50 minutes or until the filling
is set. Cool in the tin. Sprinkle with nutmeg, slice and
serve with brown sugar mascarpone (page 174). Serves 8.
▪ Peel, chop and steam 500g (1 lb) butternut pumpkin until
cooked. Cool completely and puree in a food processor.

pear and rhubarb pies

1 quantity sweet shortcrust pastry (page 157)
1 egg, beaten
raw sugar for sprinkling
filling
1/2 cup chopped rhubarb
4 brown pears (550g/181/2 oz), chopped
1/3 cup caster (superfine) sugar
2 teaspoons lemon juice
1/2 teaspoon ground cinnamon
11/2 tablespoons cornflour (cornstarch)
11/2 tablespoons water

Place the rhubarb and pear in a saucepan over medium
heat. Cover and cook, stirring occasionally, for 5 minutes.
Stir through the sugar, lemon juice and cinnamon and
simmer rapidly for 10 minutes, stirring occasionally. Mix
the cornflour and water to a paste and add to the pan.
Cook for 2 minutes or until thickened. Set aside to cool.
Preheat the oven to 200°C (400°F). Grease 6 x 1/2 cup
(4 fl oz) capacity muffin tins. Roll out the pastry on a
lightly floured surface until 3mm (1/8 in) thick. Cut out
6 x 11cm (41/2 in) rounds and line the tins. Spoon in the
cooled filling. Cut out 6 x 8cm (31/4 in) pastry rounds for
lids. Brush the rim of the bases with water, place the lids
on top and push the edges together to seal. Cut off any
excess pastry. Prick holes in the top of the pies, brush with
egg and sprinkle with sugar. Bake for 20–25 minutes or
until golden. Serve warm or cold. Makes 6.

lemon tart

1 quantity sweet shortcrust pastry (page 157)
3/4 cup (6 fl oz) lemon juice
3/4 cup caster (superfine) sugar
3/4 cup (6 fl oz) (single or pouring) cream
3 eggs, lightly beaten

Preheat the oven to 180°C (350°F). Roll out the pastry
on a lightly floured surface until 3mm (1/8 in) thick. Place
in a 22cm (9 in) fluted removable base tart tin or tart
ring*. Line the pastry with non-stick baking paper and fill
with pastry weights or uncooked rice or beans. Bake for
10 minutes, remove the weights and bake for a further
10 minutes or until the pastry is golden. Reduce the oven
temperature to 140°C (280°F).
Place the lemon juice and sugar in a heatproof bowl over
a saucepan of simmering water and stir until the sugar is
dissolved. Add the cream and eggs and stir continuously
for 5 minutes. Pour into the tart shell through a strainer.
Bake the tart for 20–25 minutes or until the filling is just
set. Cool completely and serve with thick (double) cream
or ice cream. Serves 8.

berry tartlets

375g (13 oz) ready-prepared puff pastry*
1 egg, beaten
3 teaspoons caster (superfine) sugar
brown sugar mascarpone (page 174)
500g (1 lb) mixed fresh raspberries, blueberries and strawberries

Preheat the oven to 200°C (400°F). Roll out the pastry
on a lightly floured surface to measure 30cm x 40cm
(12 in x 16 in). Cut out 12 x 9cm (31/2 in) squares and
place on two baking trays lined with non-stick baking
paper. Brush with the egg and sprinkle with the sugar.
Cover with a piece of non-stick baking paper and place
another baking tray on top to keep the pastry flat. Bake
for 15 minutes or until crisp and golden. Cool completely.
To serve, spoon some brown sugar mascarpone onto the
pastry squares and top with the berries. Serve immediately.
Makes 12.

berry tartlets

apple pie

how to apple pie

1 quantity sweet shortcrust pastry (page 157)
1 egg, lightly beaten
sugar for sprinkling
filling
8 green apples (1.2kg/2 lb 7 oz),
    peeled and chopped
1 tablespoon water
1/3 cup sugar
1 tablespoon lemon juice
1/2 teaspoon ground cinnamon
2 tablespoons almond meal

Preheat the oven to 190°C (375°F). To make the filling, place the apples and water in a deep frying pan over medium heat. Cover and simmer, shaking the pan occasionally, for 5 minutes or until just tender. Drain and cool completely. Stir in the sugar, lemon juice and cinnamon.

Divide the pastry into two-thirds and one-third. Roll out the two-thirds portion on a lightly floured surface until 3mm (1/8 in) thick and place in a shallow 24cm (9 1/2 in) pie tin. Sprinkle over the almond meal and pack the apples tightly into the pastry shell.

Roll out the remaining pastry to fit over the top of the pie. Brush the rim with water, press the edges together and trim. Cut several slits in the top of the pastry, brush with the egg and sprinkle with sugar. Bake for 30 minutes or until the pastry is golden and crisp. Serves 8.

apple and blueberry pie **Add 1 cup blueberries to the cooled apple mixture in step 1 above and continue to follow the recipe.**

apple and raspberry pie **Add 1 cup raspberries to the cooled apple mixture in step 1 above and continue to follow the recipe.**

apple and rhubarb pie **Add 1 cup chopped rhubarb to the cooled apple mixture in step 1 above and continue to follow the recipe.**

fruit mince pies

lemon meringue pie

almond tartlets

fruit mince pies

2 quantities sweet shortcrust pastry (page 157)
1 egg, lightly beaten
sugar for sprinkling
filling
1 apple (150g/5 oz), peeled and cored
1/3 cup sultanas
1/4 cup candied peel
1/3 cup currants
1/3 cup slivered almonds
1/2 cup brown sugar
1 tablespoon orange juice
3/4 teaspoon ground cinnamon
3/4 teaspoon mixed spice
pinch freshly grated nutmeg
30g (1 oz) butter, melted
1 tablespoon sherry

Grate the apple and place in a bowl with the sultanas, candied peel, currants, almonds, sugar, orange juice, cinnamon, mixed spice, nutmeg, butter and sherry. Mix well, cover and refrigerate for 24 hours.
Preheat the oven to 180°C (350°F). Roll out the pastry on a lightly floured surface until 2mm (1/8 in) thick. Cut into 7cm (2¾ in) rounds using a cookie cutter and place in shallow patty tins* or individual tart tins.
Place 3 teaspoons of fruit mixture in each tart tin. Cut stars from the remaining pastry and place on top of the fruit mixture as lids. Brush with the egg, sprinkle with sugar and bake for 12–15 minutes or until the pastry is golden and crisp. Makes 22.

almond tartlets

1/2 quantity sweet shortcrust pastry (page 157)
90g (3 oz) butter, softened
1/4 cup caster (superfine) sugar
1 egg
1 egg yolk, extra
1¼ cups almond meal
1½ tablespoons plain (all-purpose) flour
1/2 cup flaked almonds

Roll out the pastry on a lightly floured surface until 2mm (1/8 in) thick. Place in 6 x 10cm (4 in) round fluted tart tins and refrigerate for 30 minutes.
Preheat the oven to 150°C (300°F). Place the butter and sugar in the bowl of an electric mixer and beat until pale and creamy. Add the egg, egg yolk, almond meal and flour and beat until smooth. Spoon the mixture into the tart tins and smooth the tops. Sprinkle with the flaked almonds and bake for 40 minutes or until golden. Makes 6.

lemon meringue pies

1 quantity sweet shortcrust pastry (page 157)
filling
3 tablespoons cornflour (cornstarch)
1 cup (8 fl oz) water
1/2 cup sugar
1/2 cup (4 fl oz) lemon juice
2 egg yolks
60g (2 oz) butter
topping
3 egg whites
3/4 cup caster (superfine) sugar

To make the filling, place the cornflour and water in a bowl and whisk until smooth. Place the cornflour mixture, sugar and lemon juice in a saucepan over medium–high heat and whisk until the mixture boils, then boil for 5 minutes or until it thickens. Remove from the heat and stir through the egg yolks and butter. Set aside to cool slightly.
Preheat the oven to 180°C (350°F). Roll out the pastry on a lightly floured surface until 3mm (1/8 in) thick. Cut out rounds to fit 6 x 9cm (3½ in) round pie tins. Place in the base of the tins, line with non-stick baking paper and fill with pastry weights or uncooked rice or beans. Bake for 10 minutes, remove the weights and bake for a further 10 minutes or until the pastry is golden. Pour the cooled filling into the pastry shells and refrigerate for 1 hour or until set.
To make the topping, place the egg whites in a bowl and beat until soft peaks form. Add the sugar gradually and beat until the mixture is thick and glossy. Spoon on top of the filled pies and place under a hot grill (broiler) for 1 minute or until the meringue is set and golden. Makes 6.

free-form peach and plum pie

1 quantity sweet shortcrust pastry (page 157)
1/4 cup almond meal
4 ripe peaches, stoned and cut into wedges
4 blood plums, stoned and cut into wedges
1 tablespoon sugar

Preheat the oven to 180°C (350°F). Roll out the pastry on a lightly floured surface into a rough circle 3mm (1/8 in) thick and place on a baking tray lined with non-stick baking paper. Sprinkle the pastry with the almond meal, leaving a 5cm (2 in) border. Place the peach and plum wedges on top and sprinkle over the sugar. Fold the sides of the pastry up to partially enclose the fruit. Refrigerate for 10 minutes.
Bake for 45 minutes or until golden brown. Serve warm with thick (double) cream or ice cream. Serves 6–8.

free-form peach and plum pie

custard tarts

1 quantity sweet shortcrust pastry (page 157)
1 cup (8 fl oz) milk
1 cup (8 fl oz) (single or pouring) cream
1 vanilla bean*, split and scraped
3 eggs
3 egg yolks, extra
1/2 cup caster (superfine) sugar
freshly grated nutmeg for sprinkling

Preheat the oven to 180°C (350°F). Roll out the pastry on a lightly floured surface until 3mm (1/8 in) thick. Place in the base of 6 x 9cm (3 1/2 in) pie tins, line with non-stick baking paper and fill with pastry weights or uncooked rice or beans. Bake for 10 minutes, remove the weights and bake for a further 10 minutes or until the pastry is golden. Reduce the oven temperature to 140°C (280°F). Place the milk, cream and vanilla bean in a saucepan over medium heat. Bring to the boil, remove from the heat and set aside. Place the eggs, extra egg yolks and sugar in a bowl and whisk until pale and thick. Remove the vanilla bean from the milk mixture and gradually whisk into the egg mixture. Pour the filling into the tart cases through a strainer. Sprinkle with nutmeg and bake for 20–25 minutes or until just set. Set aside for 5 minutes before serving. Makes 6.

pecan pie

1 quantity sweet shortcrust pastry (page 157)
1 cup pecan nuts
1/2 cup brown sugar
1/2 cup maple syrup
40g (1 1/2 oz) butter, melted and cooled
3 eggs
1/4 cup (2 fl oz) (single or pouring) cream

Preheat the oven to 180°C (350°F). Roll out the pastry on a lightly floured surface until 3mm (1/8 in) thick. Place in a 22cm (9 in) fluted removable base tart tin*. Line with non-stick baking paper and fill with pastry weights or uncooked rice or beans. Bake for 10 minutes, remove the weights and bake for a further 10 minutes or until the pastry is golden. Place the pecans on a baking tray and bake for 5 minutes. Set aside to cool completely.
Reduce the oven temperature to 160°C (325°F). Place the sugar, maple syrup, butter, eggs and cream in a bowl and whisk to combine. Stir through the pecans. Pour into the tart shell and bake for 35 minutes or until the filling is set. Cool before serving. Serves 8.

chocolate tart

1 quantity hazelnut sweet shortcrust pastry (page 157)
7 egg yolks
2 tablespoons caster (superfine) sugar
2 1/3 cups (18 1/2 fl oz) (single or pouring) cream
200g (7 oz) dark chocolate, chopped

Preheat the oven to 180°C (350°F). Roll out the pastry on a lightly floured surface until 3mm (1/8 in) thick. Place in a 26cm (10 in) fluted removable base tart tin*. Line with non-stick baking paper and fill with pastry weights or uncooked rice or beans. Bake for 10 minutes, remove the weights and bake for a further 10 minutes or until the pastry is golden. Reduce the oven temperature to 150°C (300°F). Place the egg yolks and sugar in a bowl and whisk until the sugar is dissolved. Place the cream in a saucepan over medium heat, bring just to the boil and remove from the heat. Add the chocolate and stir until smooth. Pour over the egg yolk mixture and stir to combine. Pour into the tart shell and bake for 15–20 minutes or until just set. Cool completely before serving in wedges with thick (double) cream and berries if desired. Serves 10–12.

peach tart

1 quantity sweet shortcrust pastry (page 157)
3/4 cup sour cream
2 tablespoons caster (superfine) sugar
1 egg
1 egg white, extra
1 tablespoon sugar
6 peaches, stoned and sliced
1 tablespoon sugar, extra, for sprinkling

Preheat the oven to 180°C (350°F). Roll out the pastry on a lightly floured surface until 3mm (1/8 in) thick. Place in a 23cm (9 in) fluted removable base tart tin*. Line with non-stick baking paper and fill with pastry weights or uncooked rice or beans. Bake for 10 minutes, remove the weights and bake for a further 10 minutes or until the pastry is golden. Place the sour cream, caster sugar and egg in a bowl and whisk to combine. Pour into the tart shell and bake for 10 minutes. Remove from the oven and increase the temperature to 200°C (400°F). Place the egg white in a large bowl and whisk until soft peaks form. Stir through the sugar and peach slices until coated then spoon on top of the cream filling. Sprinkle with the extra sugar and bake for 20 minutes or until golden. Cool completely before serving. Serve with thick (double) cream. Serves 6–8.

custard tarts

chocolate tart

pecan pie

peach tart

how to apple tarte tatin

60g (2 oz) butter
3/4 cup caster (superfine) sugar
2 tablespoons water
4 Granny Smith apples (600g/20 oz),
   peeled, cored and quartered
375g (13 oz) ready-prepared puff pastry*

Preheat the oven to 200°C (400°F). Place an 18cm (7 in) frying pan with an ovenproof handle over medium heat. Add the butter and allow to melt. Add the sugar and water and cook, stirring, for 2 minutes or until the sugar is dissolved. Continue to cook for 5 minutes or until light golden and syrupy.

Add the apples to the pan and cook for 5 minutes. Allow the bubbles to subside then arrange the apple pieces in a circular pattern, core-side up, over the base of the frying pan.

Roll out the pastry on a lightly floured surface until 3mm (1/8 in) thick. Cut out a 24cm (9 1/2 in) circle and place over the apples, tucking the edge under. Bake for 18–20 minutes or until the pastry is puffed and golden. To serve, invert the tart onto a plate and slice into wedges. Serve with thick (double) cream. Serves 4–6.

pear tarte tatin **Replace the apples with 4 peeled, cored and quartered firm pears. Add to the pan in step 2 above, cook for 3–4 minutes, then continue with the recipe.**
apricot tarte tatin **Replace the apples with 8–10 halved and stoned apricots. Add to the pan in step 2 above, cook for 1–2 minutes or until just softened, then continue with the recipe.**

apple tarte tatin

short order

apricot turnovers

tart and bun glaze

fruit galettes

short order

apricot turnovers

Preheat the oven to 200°C (400°F). Cut ready-prepared and rolled puff pastry* into rounds and place on a baking tray lined with non-stick baking paper. Place drained canned apricot halves on one half of the pastry. Sprinkle with sugar, brush the edges with milk, fold over and fork the edges together. Brush with milk, sprinkle with sugar and bake for 25 minutes or until golden. Makes 4.

tart and bun glaze

Place 1/2 cup sugar and 1/4 cup (2 fl oz) water in a small saucepan over low heat, stirring until the sugar is dissolved. Remove any sugar crystals on the side with a pastry brush dipped in water. Add 2 teaspoons powdered gelatine sprinkled over 1 tablespoon water and cook for 1 minute. Set aside to cool. Brush over tarts filled with crème pâtissière and berries or over buns. Refrigerate to set.

fruit galettes

Preheat the oven to 200°C (400°F). Roll out 375g (13 oz) ready-prepared puff pastry* on a lightly floured surface until 2mm (1/8 in) thick. Cut into rectangles and place on a baking tray lined with non-stick baking paper. Top with thinly sliced apple, pear, peach or nectarine. Sprinkle with sugar and bake for 20 minutes or until golden.

breakfast Danish

Preheat the oven to 200°C (400°F). Roll out 375g (13 oz) ready-prepared puff pastry* on a lightly floured surface until 5mm (1/4 in) thick. Cut out 4 x 12cm (5 in) squares and place on a baking tray lined with non-stick baking paper. Sprinkle with 2 tablespoons shredded coconut. Combine 1 chopped banana, 2 tablespoons passionfruit pulp and 1 tablespoon caster (superfine) sugar. Place in the middle of the pastry, brush the edges with milk and pinch together. Brush with milk, sprinkle with sugar and bake for 20 minutes or until golden.

brown sugar mascarpone

Combine 2 cups mascarpone* and 1/2 cup brown sugar in a bowl. Spoon into a baked tart shell and top with fruit or serve on the side with other desserts.

crème pâtissière

Place 2 cups (16 fl oz) milk and 1 teaspoon vanilla extract in a saucepan over medium–high heat and bring to the boil. Whisk together 4 egg yolks and 1/3 cup caster (superfine) sugar until thick and pale. Add 1/3 cup cornflour (cornstarch) and whisk to combine. Slowly pour in the hot milk, whisking continuously. Pour the mixture back into the saucepan over medium–high heat and simmer rapidly while whisking continuously for 5 minutes or until thick. Place a piece of non-stick baking paper or plastic wrap directly onto the surface of the pastry cream to cover it and set aside to cool. Spoon into baked tart shells and top with fruit or use to fill doughnuts or cakes. Makes 2 1/3 cups.

macaroon pastry cases

Preheat the oven to 150°C (300°F). Combine 1 3/4 cups desiccated coconut, 1/2 cup caster (superfine) sugar and 2 egg whites in a bowl. Grease 6 x 10cm (4 in) fluted removable base tart tins*. Press the mixture into the tins and bake for 30 minutes or until golden. Cool and fill with lemon, orange or passionfruit curd (page 124) or chocolate mousse (page 106). Makes 6.

fruit almond tarts

Preheat the oven to 150°C (300°F) Make the almond tartlet filling from page 166. Grease 4 x 10cm (4 in) round tart tins and spoon in the filling. Smooth the tops and sprinkle over 1/2 cup raspberries or blueberries instead of the flaked almonds. Gently press the berries into the filling, sprinkle with icing (confectioner's) sugar and bake for 35–40 minutes or until golden. Makes 4.

breakfast Danish

brown sugar mascarpone

crème pâtissière

macaroon pastry cases

fruit almond tarts

tools

Get your tins in order, stock up on the essential ingredients, and you've covered the basic tools of the baking trade. Invest in a few whisks, wooden and metal spoons, bowls and spatulas, a roll or two of non-stick baking paper and a pair of electric beaters or an electric mixer. A food processor or blender is handy, and an oven, of course, is essential – plus an oven thermometer to check it is cooking at the right temperature. As far as tins go, whether you are a regular cake-maker or just a beginner, aluminium tins are fine but stainless steel will last longer and won't warp or buckle. Measure tin widths at the open top, not at the base. If the tin has a lip, take the measurement from the inside of the lip.

square, slice and loaf tins

square tins The standard sizes for square tins are 18cm, 20cm, 22cm and 24cm (7 in, 8 in, 9 in and 9$\frac{1}{2}$ in). If you have a recipe for a cake cooked in a round tin and you want to use a square tin, the general rule is to subtract 2cm (about 1 in) from the size of the tin. So you would need a 20cm (8 in) square cake tin for a recipe calling for a 22cm (9 in) round cake tin.
slice tins The standard size is 20cm x 30cm (8 in x 12 in). These tins are great for slices or large slab cakes.
loaf tins The standard size is 10cm x 20cm (4 in x 8 in), although a longer and more narrow tin can also be great to set jellies (jello) and other desserts in.

muffin and patty tins

muffin tins The standard sizes are a 12 hole tin, each hole with $\frac{1}{2}$ cup (4 fl oz) capacity, or a 6 hole tin, each hole with 1 cup (8 fl oz) capacity. Great for making individual cakes and muffins. Non-stick tins make for easy removal, or line with paper patty cases.
patty tins These come in a variety of sizes but the standard is 2 tablespoon capacity. There are also shallow patty tins which are great for small tarts and pies. Grease the tins well before using or line them with paper patty cases for easy removal.

fancy tins

angel food cake tin It may seem excessive to buy a cake tin that is specially designed for just one kind of cake, but this cake really does work best in this particular tin. You could use a deep ring tin if an angel food cake tin was not available.
fluted ring tins Bundt and kugelhopf are two of the many varieties available. Whatever the shape, always grease a fluted tin well. To remove a cake from one, loosen it with a palette knife and give it a slight twist.
madeleine tins Another speciality tin designed for just one recipe, but taste one of these little light-as-air cakes and you'll happily invest in one. Because of their delicate shell shape, madeleines do have a tendency to stick, so grease and flour the tins or spray with non-stick cooking spray.

round and springform tins

round tins The standard sizes for round tins are 18cm, 20cm, 22cm and 24cm (7 in, 8 in, 9 in and 9$\frac{1}{2}$ in). The 20cm and 24cm (8 in and 9$\frac{1}{2}$ in) round tins are the must-haves of the range.
springform tins The standard sizes are 20cm, 22cm and 24cm (8 in, 9 in and 9$\frac{1}{2}$ in). The best tin to use for delicate cakes such as cheesecakes, mud cakes and layer cakes. The spring-loaded side collar lifts away, allowing for removal of the cake without the need to invert.

tart tins and rings

fluted tart tins Are available in individual-serve to large sizes, may be deep or shallow, and come with or without removable bases. The standard sizes are 10cm, 20cm and 24cm (4 in, 8 in and 9$\frac{1}{2}$ in). Opt for the removable base for easy removal of delicate crusts, especially when using a larger tart tin.
tart rings These metal rings sit flat on a lined baking tray and are used for cooking tarts with a straight side. Simply lift the ring away at the end of baking. Available from speciality cookware shops.

square, slice and loaf tins

muffin and patty tins

round and springform tins

fancy tins

tart tins and rings

179

sugar

butter

eggs

cream

flavours

sugar

regular granulated white sugar is used in baking when a light texture is not crucial to the outcome. Because its crystals are quite large, you need to beat, add liquids and heat regular sugar to dissolve it.

caster (superfine) sugar gives baked products a light texture and crumb, which is important with most cakes and light desserts such as meringue and zabaglione.

brown sugar is sugar that has been processed with molasses. It comes in differing shades of brown, according to the quantity of molasses added, which varies between countries. This also affects the taste of the sugar, and therefore the end product. The brown sugar referred to in this book is sometimes also called light brown sugar. For a richer taste you can substitute dark brown sugar.

icing (confectioner's) sugar is regular granulated sugar ground to a very fine powder. It often clumps together and needs to be pressed through a fine sieve before using. Always use pure icing (confectioner's) sugar not an icing sugar mixture, which will contain cornflour (cornstarch).

demerara sugar See page 186.

butter

for cakes Unless stated otherwise in a recipe, butter should be at room temperature for cooking. It should not be half-melted or too soft to handle, however, but still have some 'give' when pressed.

for pastry When using butter to make pastry, it should be cold and chopped into small pieces so that it can be evenly distributed throughout the flour.

salted or unsalted Although most bakers use unsalted rather than salted butter, it is a matter of personal preference and does not make much difference to the outcome. Salted butter has a much longer shelf-life, which makes it preferable for some people. Store butter in the fridge away from other foods with odours, mild or strong, as it is very easily tainted.

eggs

size The standard egg size used in this book is 59g (2 oz). It is very important to use the right size eggs for a recipe, as this will affect the outcome of baked goods. The correct volume is especially important when using egg whites for meringues.

temperature Use eggs at room temperature for baking. Remove them from the fridge about 30 minutes before you begin.

cream

single or pouring cream has a butter fat content of 20–30 per cent. It is the type of cream most commonly used for making ice cream, panna cotta and custard. It can also be whipped to a light and airy consistency and served on the side.

thickened cream (not to be mistaken for thick cream, below) is single or pouring cream that has had a vegetable gum added to stabilise it. The gum makes the cream a little thicker and easier to whip.

thick (double) cream has a butter fat content of 40–50 per cent. It is usually served on the side or on top of cakes and desserts.

flavourings

chocolate The most important rule when cooking with chocolate is: the better the quality, the better the result. Avoid using compound chocolate, which has inferior taste. For dark chocolate, use a couverture variety (see page 186) that contains 54–57 per cent cocoa solids. For a more bitter chocolate taste, use a couverture chocolate with 64 per cent cocoa solids, but note that it will affect the texture of the cake or dessert, making it more dense.

cocoa powder Use a non-alkalised or good-quality processed Dutch cocoa powder (available from speciality cooking shops and delicatessens) for good flavour and results.

vanilla There are many different forms of vanilla flavouring. For a pure and perfect vanilla taste, use a good-quality vanilla extract, not an essence or imitation flavour, or use a vanilla bean (see page 186).

before you start

greasing a cake tin

To grease a cake tin, brush a little melted butter over the inside. You can also dust the buttered tin with some flour, tapping away the excess. Be sure to butter the tin well where the side meets the base, and around the middle section of a ring tin.

lining a cake tin

To guarantee easy removal of a cake every time, line the base of the tin with one piece of non-stick baking paper (the silicone coating gives good results), and the side with another.

preheating the oven

Allow the oven to heat for at least 15–20 minutes before placing your cake, slice, biscuits, cookies or puddings in to bake.

creaming butter and sugar

It takes around 4–5 minutes to beat together butter and sugar to a creamy consistency using an electric mixer. A mixture is properly creamed when it becomes lighter than the yellow colour of butter – a pale cream – and the sugar is partly dissolved. If the butter and sugar are not creamed sufficiently, the resulting cake will not have a light texture and may also have white spots on the surface because the sugar has not been incorporated properly.

beating eggs

When making most cakes, you will need to add the eggs gradually – one at a time, and beat well between each addition. This is essential to a cake's success, as eggs are often used to bind the mixture together, and need to be very well distributed to do this. Always do this step slowly and thoroughly for a good outcome.

separating eggs

When separating eggs, do each one individually over a separate bowl in case a yolk breaks and taints the whites. As for the method, practice makes perfect.

folding

When a recipe calls for ingredients to be folded through, use a large metal spoon to carefully make cutting, turning and folding over motions through the mixture (a rubber spatula or wooden spoon creates too much drag). The principle behind folding is to not over-mix, maintaining the air that has been beaten in previously for a lightly textured outcome.

soft peaks

When instructed to beat egg whites until soft peaks form, lift the beaters or whisk out, and the point where they leave the mixture – the peak – should fall softly back onto itself.

stiff peaks

When instructed to beat egg whites until stiff peaks form, lift the beaters or whisk out, and the point where they leave the mixture – the peak – should stand upright. It is easy to over-beat egg whites at this stage, so check frequently. Over-beaten egg whites will appear grainy and dry.

measuring ingredients

For dry ingredients, it is best to use measuring cups or scales. For an accurate measure when using cups, spoon the ingredients into the cup and then level off with the back of a knife. Never scoop the cup directly into the ingredients or pack down the ingredients into the cup (except in the case of brown sugar, which is sticky and needs to be pressed in).

When measuring with scales, be sure to 'tare', or have the scales at zero, with the empty bowl or vessel in place and then add the ingredients to be measured. When measuring liquids, always use a jug and check the measure at eye level, not from above.

even cooking

For an evenly baked cake, slice, biscuit or cookie, set your oven timer for half the time required by the recipe, then turn the cake tin or baking tray around and set the timer for the remaining time.

a level oven

If your cakes come out of the oven with an unexplained lean, check whether the oven is sitting level using a spirit level.

oven temperatures

Before you blame a recipe or your cooking skills for a failed cake or an under- or overcooked pudding, check the true temperature of your oven, which can be very different to what the dial is saying. To do this, preheat your oven as the recipe indicates, then place an oven thermometer (inexpensive and available from department stores) on the middle shelf in the middle of the oven, and readjust the temperature accordingly.

sugar syrup and caramel

When making sugar syrup or caramel from sugar and water, it is important to stir the mixture so that the sugar dissolves before the mixture bubbles. Also, wipe down the inside of the saucepan with a pastry brush that has been dipped into water to remove any sugar crystals. This will help to give you a clear syrup that will not crystallise.

a perfect finish

removing a cake from a tin
For easy removal, run a palette knife gently between the edge of the cooked cake and the tin. Invert the tin onto a wire rack, allowing the cake to gently fall onto it. Place a plate or another rack on the cake and turn it the right way up if necessary.
To remove a small cake from its tin, run a palette knife around the edge of the cake or simply give it a little twist to remove it. This should be simple if the tin is a non-stick one and/or has been well prepared – either greased or lined with baking paper.

straightening a cake
If your cake comes out of the oven with a peaked top or oddly shaped top, just camouflage the imperfection. Allow the cake to cool then carefully slice the top with a serrated-edge knife. Brush away any crumbs then spread over some icing.

cooling a cake
Unless stated in a recipe that it needs to cool in the tin, a cake is best cooled quickly on a wire rack. If left in the tin, the base of the cake may become soggy or, in the case of cakes with a high sugar content, stick to the tin.

a perfectly glazed cake
When making a chocolate glaze, do not stir it too much. Excessive stirring adds air bubbles, which will inhibit a perfectly smooth finish. Refrigerate the cake for at least 30 minutes before spreading on the glaze. Then place the cake on a wire rack with a tray underneath to catch the excess glaze. Brush the cake with a soft pastry brush to remove any crumbs. Pour the glaze over the cake and allow it to run down the sides.

Tap the rack gently on the bench to remove any air bubbles. The chill of the cake will be enough to set the glaze perfectly. If the weather is warm, store the cake in the warmest place in the fridge. Storing the cake in a very cold place will make the glaze appear dull.

a perfectly iced cake
Refrigerate the cake for at least 30 minutes before spreading on the icing. A simple icing made with icing (confectioner's) sugar should be of a spreadable consistency. Test this by placing a small amount on the cake; the icing should start to spread slightly on its own but not be so thin that you can see the cake through it. Adjust the icing with more icing sugar or water if necessary before you begin. Place the chilled cake on a wire rack with a tray underneath to catch any excess icing. Brush the cake with a soft pastry brush to remove any crumbs. Spoon the icing over the middle of the cake then spread with a palette knife and allow the icing to drip over the edges. If you wish to cover the side of the cake, place a small amount of icing on the palette knife and run it around the side. Allow any excess icing to run off and stand the cake for 10 minutes to allow the icing to set.

a perfectly frosted cake
Refrigerate the cake for at least 30 minutes and place on a wire rack. Large, even strokes with a flat palette knife are the best way to achieve a smooth finish with a thick frosting such as a cream cheese or chocolate frosting. Spoon a large amount of frosting on the middle of the cake and work it towards the edge with a palette knife using large sweeping

motions. Spread some frosting roughly around the side of the cake, then, with the palette knife vertical, run it in one continuous sweep around the cake for a perfectly smooth side. You could also create a swirled and textured frosting finish.

simple piping bag
Take a small regular or snap-top plastic bag and fill it with icing or cream then snip off one corner when you are ready to ice your cake.

storing a cake
Generally, cakes with a higher fat content keep better and often improve over a few days (chocolate mud cake, for example). Cakes with a finer texture and less fat, such as a sponge cake, need to be eaten on the day they are made. Store all cakes in an airtight container. Store cakes containing fresh ingredients such as cream or cream cheese in the fridge.

storing biscuits and cookies
Store biscuits and cookies in airtight containers. To keep cookies and biscuits crisp, store them between layers of absorbent paper towel, which will soak up any moisture.

whipping cream
In warm weather it is best to whip cream over a bowl of iced water. This will keep the cream cool and minimise the chance of it splitting.

dusting
When dusting a cake or dessert with icing (confectioner's) sugar or cocoa powder, use a very fine sieve to get rid of the lumps and distribute the powder evenly. Dust with icing sugar or cocoa just before serving, as they may be absorbed into the cake.

glossary

amaretti
Italian biscuits based on ground almonds, traditionally using bitter almonds. Available from many delicatessens. See page 36 to make your own.

angel food cake tin
See Tools, page 178.

brioche
A sweet French yeast bread made in loaf or bun form. Traditionally dunked in coffee at breakfast. Available from speciality bread and cake stores and some supermarkets. See page 56 to make your own.

couverture chocolate
Available from speciality food stores and some delicatessens. Dark couverture chocolate is preferred for cooking. Milk couverture chocolate is available but can be substituted with good-quality eating chocolate. See Tools, page 181, for more details.

cream
See Tools, page 181.

demerara sugar
A brown, crystallised cane sugar with a mild caramel flavour. Suitable for use in cooking. Available from speciality food stores and most supermarkets. If unavailable, substitute with 3 parts white sugar mixed with 1 part brown sugar.

fluted bundt tin
See Tools, page 178.

fluted ring tin
See Tools, page 178.

framboise
A raspberry-flavoured brandy.

hazelnut meal
Available from many supermarkets or make your own by processing whole skinned hazelnuts to a fine meal in a food processor or blender (130g/4 oz whole hazelnuts will give 1 cup hazelnut meal). To remove the skins from whole hazelnuts, wrap in a tea towel and rub vigorously.

madeleine tins
See Tools, page 178.

mascarpone
A fresh Italian triple-cream curd-style cheese. Its consistency is similar to thick (double) cream and it is used in a similar way. Available from speciality food stores and many delicatessens and supermarkets.

panettone or pandoro
Light and airy long-life Italian Christmas 'cake' with a bread-like consistency. Available plain and in other flavours, with or without fruit, from delicatessens.

patty tins
See Tools, page 178.

puff pastry
Time-consuming to make. Available from patisseries (order a block in advance) or use the ready-prepared frozen supermarket variety, in block form if possible, so you can roll it out to the thickness you need. If buying ready-prepared puff pastry sheets, you may need to layer several to get the required thickness.

ramekins
Small ovenproof dishes usually made from porcelain and used to cook and serve dishes such as soufflés, crème brûlèe and fruit crumbles.

removable base tart tin or ring
See Tools, page 178.

rice paper
Edible wrapping used traditionally in Italian sweet cookery, especially when making panforte. Available from Italian delicatessens and speciality food stores.

sponge finger biscuits
Sweet and light Italian finger-shaped biscuits, also known as savoiardi. Great for desserts such as tiramisu because they absorb other flavours and soften well but maintain their shape. Available from delicatessens and most supermarkets.

springform tin
See Tools, page 178.

sugar (candy) thermometer
A kitchen thermometer used to test the temperature of sugar syrup, jams and jellies during cooking. Marked according to the consistency of sugar syrup for sweet (candy) making. Available from speciality cookware and department stores.

sweet shortcrust pastry
See page 157.

vanilla beans
These cured pods from the vanilla orchid are used whole, and often split and the tiny beans scraped into the mixture, to infuse flavour into custard and cream-based recipes. Available from speciality food stores, delicatessens and supermarkets. If unavailable, substitute 1 vanilla bean with 1 teaspoon pure vanilla extract (a dark, thick, sticky liquid – not vanilla essence).

conversion chart

1 teaspoon = 5 ml
1 Australian tablespoon = 20 ml
   (4 teaspoons)
1 UK tablespoon = 15 ml
   (3 teaspoons/$1/2$ fl oz)
1 cup = 250 ml (8 fl oz)

liquid conversions

metric	imperial	US cups
30 ml	1 fl oz	$1/8$ cup
60 ml	2 fl oz	$1/4$ cup
80 ml	$2^{3/4}$ fl oz	$1/3$ cup
125 ml	4 fl oz	$1/2$ cup
185 ml	6 fl oz	$3/4$ cup
250 ml	8 fl oz	1 cup
375 ml	12 fl oz	$1^{1/2}$ cups
500 ml	16 fl oz	2 cups
600 ml	20 fl oz	$2^{1/2}$ cups
750 ml	24 fl oz	3 cups
1 litre	32 fl oz	4 cups

cup measures

1 cup almond meal	110g	$3^{1/2}$ oz	1 cup lemon rind, shredded	50g	$1^{1/2}$ oz
1 cup almonds, blanched	170g	$5^{1/2}$ oz	1 cup lime rind, shredded	50g	$1^{1/2}$ oz
1 cup almonds, flaked	125g	4 oz	1 cup malted milk powder	130g	4 oz
1 cup almonds, slivered	140g	$4^{1/2}$ oz	1 cup maple syrup	380g	13 oz
1 cup apples, dried	100g	$3^{1/2}$ oz	1 cup mixed peel, candied	190g	$6^{1/2}$ oz
1 cup apricots, dried	190g	$6^{1/2}$ oz	1 cup orange rind, shredded	50g	$1^{1/2}$ oz
1 cup banana, mashed	240g	$7^{1/2}$ oz	1 cup peaches, dried	200g	7 oz
1 cup blueberries, fresh	125g	4 oz	1 cup pecan nuts, chopped	110g	$3^{1/2}$ oz
1 cup blueberries, frozen	125g	4 oz	1 cup poppy seeds	150g	5 oz
1 cup carrot, grated	115g	$3^{1/2}$ oz	1 cup prunes	200g	7 oz
1 cup caster (superfine) sugar	225g	$7^{1/2}$ oz	1 cup raisins	200g	7 oz
1 cup chocolate, chopped	150g	5 oz	1 cup raspberries, fresh	125g	4 oz
1 cup cocoa powder	115g	$3^{1/2}$ oz	1 cup raspberries, frozen	125g	4 oz
1 cup coconut, desiccated	90g	3 oz	1 cup raspberry jam (jelly)	350g	12 oz
1 cup coconut, shredded	90g	3 oz	1 cup redcurrants	120g	4 oz
1 cup cornflour (cornstarch)	100g	$3^{1/2}$ oz	1 cup rhubarb, chopped	120g	4 oz
1 cup cream, thick (double)	250g	8 oz	1 cup rice flour	100g	$3^{1/2}$ oz
1 cup currants	150g	5 oz	1 cup rolled oats, uncooked	100g	$3^{1/2}$ oz
1 cup dates, chopped	160g	$5^{1/2}$ oz	1 cup sour cream	250g	8 oz
1 cup flour, plain	135g	$4^{1/2}$ oz	1 cup sugar, brown	200g	7 oz
1 cup glacé ginger, chopped	240g	$7^{1/2}$ oz	1 cup sugar, caster (superfine)	225g	$7^{1/2}$ oz
1 cup golden syrup	380g	13 oz	1 cup sugar, white	225g	$7^{1/2}$ oz
1 cup hazelnuts, whole	130g	4 oz	1 cup sultanas	200g	7 oz
1 cup honey	400g	14 oz	1 cup thick (double) cream	250g	8 oz
1 cup icing (confectioner's) sugar	125g	4 oz	1 cup walnuts, chopped	140g	$4^{1/2}$ oz

index